IT Infrastructure Library

Service Level Management

Customer focused

Jan Niessen
Paul Oldenburg

LONDON: THE
STATIONERY OFFICE

Central Computer and Telecommunications Agency

'ITIL' and 'Information Technology Infrastructure Library' are registered trademarks of CCTA.

CCTA
Rosebery Court
St Andrews Business Park
Norwich
NR7 0HS
UK

Tel: (+44/0) 1603 704704
email: info@ccta.gov.uk

Contents

		Foreword	5
		Acknowledgements	7
1		**Introduction**	**9**
	1.1	What is service level management	9
	1.2	Purpose	10
	1.3	Structure	10
	1.4	Target readership	11
	1.5	Context	11
	1.6	Related guidance	12
	1.7	Benefits, costs and possible problems	13
2		**The service level management process**	**17**
	2.1	Introduction	17
	2.2	Goal	17
	2.3	Results	17
	2.4	Scope	17
	2.5	Activities	19
	2.6	Relationships	30
	2.7	Roles and responsibilities	36
3		**Quantifying IT services**	**39**
	3.1	Why quantify IT services?	39
	3.2	Approach	39
	3.3	The customer	40
	3.4	Identifying service level requirements	40
	3.5	Specifying service levels	42
	3.6	Producing the documents	55
4		**The Service Quality Plan**	**61**
	4.1	Introduction to the Service Quality Plan	61
	4.2	Internal targets	63
	4.3	Underpinning contracts	65
	4.4	Operational level agreements	66
	4.5	Defining the Service Quality Plan	66
	4.6	Building the Service Quality Plan document	67
	4.7	Maintaining the Service Quality Plan	68

Annex A	Further information and associated guidance	71
Annex B	Bibliography	73
Annex C	Glossary	75
Annex D	Skeletons	77
Annex E	Self assessment	95
Annex F	Awareness campaign	99
Annex G	Do's and don'ts of service level management	105

Foreword

Welcome to the IT Infrastructure Library (ITIL) book *Service Level Management – customer focused*. This book is a revision and replacement of the ITIL Service Level Management book that first appeared in 1989. As with all ITIL books developed under EXIN's management, this book has had many contributors who have given up their time and shared their knowledge and experience to ensure that the contents are as comprehensive, accurate and useful as possible. Throughout the development process, the views of the authors have been, by turn, constrained, expanded, questioned, encouraged, supported and tested. Such breadth of input is vital to retaining the wide applicability and non-proprietary nature of the ITIL products.

The customer focused view of Service Level Management (SLM) takes the needs of the customer for IT services and agrees them in a measurable way, expressing those requirements, and the measurements that describe them, in terms meaningful to the business. These business requirements are then interpreted in terms of the internal target and measurements required to assemble and deliver the IT services support that the business needs. This translation role is by no means a trivial task, but is perhaps the key element of successful IT service management.

This book differs from its predecessor in many ways – driven by experience, changing technical environments and by culture – but mostly by its commitment to a customer focused approach. The guidance in this book encourages the IT services organisation to start from the customers' needs and to construct and monitor IT delivery in such a way as to achieve those service targets within agreed cost and other constraints. This approach is possible only by building upon earlier SLM guidance; the change in culture has been made possible by organisations implementing the guidance contained in the earlier version – without that start we could not now be taking the SLM concept forward.

Customer focus is the key message that pervades modern IT service management. As IT service management becomes ever more widely recognised as a key skill required by all successful organisations, so it develops and matures as a profession.

Research into service level management undertaken by CCTA (with Pink Elephant) in producing the ITIL Business Perspective books provided an initial move towards a more customer-focused ITIL.

This progress is reflected throughout the elements that make up the 'ITIL philosophy' – not only in the increasing numbers holding professional qualifications via EXIN and ISEB, but also in the growing membership base of ITSMF organisations. Perhaps more important still is the growing acceptance of and demand for these qualifications by employers, and in the growing number of customer organisations encouraging their staff to be active members of relevant user groups.

In summary, the future looks good for ITIL, but only while it accurately reflects, and leads, the requirements and best practice for IT service management. The revision exercise is vital and this book therefore marks an important stage in the ongoing development of ITIL and IT service management.

Ivor Macfarlane– ITIL Product Manager, EXIN

Acknowledgements

The authors, Jan Niessen and Paul Oldenburg are both senior consultants with Syntegra, the systems integration business of BT.

Thanks are due to the following people for their valuable contributions during the quality assurance of this book.

Professor Margaret van Biene-Hershey	Vrije Universiteit Amsterdam
Pippa Craddock	ITSMF
Paul Crone	A V Holding
Neville Greenhalgh	Proof reader
Ivor Macfarlane	EXIN
Bob Prescott-Jones	EDS
Frances Scarff	CCTA
Albert Schotanus	Cap Gemini
Ruud de Vreugd	Scheepvaartinspectie
Bart Westra	Interpay
David Wheeldon	Ultracomp

Ted Jackson and Liz Longbottom of LEJEN Consultants for work on the structure and layout of the book.

1 Introduction

1.1 What is service level management

Service level management (SLM) is the process of managing a delivered IT service, in terms of quality, quantity and cost. Today, this service level management process must take place in the light of an ever-changing business need, and is underpinned by changing technology. By its nature, the process is a compromise between the quality and quantity of the delivered service and its cost, establishing the key role of the Service Level Manager in achieving the balance the organisation requires. Crucial to success is the recognition by all parties, supplier and customer, that a service is, in fact, being supplied and received; recognition of this is formalised by the preparation, agreement and maintenance of formal SLAs which document all the relevant details of an IT service.

The service level management process can be seen as the 'bridge' between customer and supplier, which:

- integrates the disparate elements that make up service provision

- packages them into an easily used and understood service

- expresses that service in terms the customer can understand, ie in business terms.

This positioning of service level management shows its key role in the IT service management process, emphasising its close connection with the other customer facing functions, including the help desk and customer liaison.

Like a ship, the SLM function can be seen as having two parts – above and below the waterline. Above the waterline are services the customers need, expressed in their terms; below the waterline are the technical means and mechanisms for achieving those services. Most customers will neither be able to, nor would want to, understand the technical aspects. A good service level management function should administer the technical assets and support business needs, keeping technical aspects out of sight 'under the water', their invisibility to the customer being a measure of SLM's success.

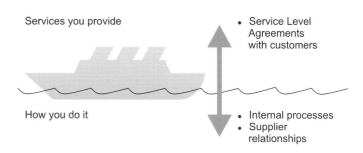

Figure 1: The waterline

1.2 Purpose

This book sets out to help organisations make the service level management process work for them and for their customers. This is achieved via three stages:

- describing the theoretical contents of the service level management process

- defining and quantifying the IT services supporting customers

- guidance on establishing a Service Quality Plan.

This book has been designed as a workbook, to be frequently off the shelf and open on the desk. To help in achieving best practice, Annex D contains several skeleton documents: project plan, Service Catalogue, SLA, underpinning contract and a number of specification sheets.

Customers
Throughout this book, the customer is considered to be the recipient of the IT service. Usually the customer will have responsibility for the cost of the IT service either directly through charging or indirectly in terms of demonstrable business need.

1.3 Structure

Chapter 2 defines the service level management process in terms of the process goal, activities, results and feedback mechanism. The relationships with other IT processes are discussed, and guidance is given on how to organise the SLM process, and to define the associated roles and responsibilities.

In Chapter 3 the challenge of defining IT services is met. Frequently asked questions are answered, such as:

- how can an IT service be defined, using the vocabulary of the customer?

- how can we quantify the services and develop meaningful external metrics?

- how can we translate those metrics into internal requirements and targets?

Chapter 4 discusses the concept of a Service Quality Plan. Establishing such a plan is the department's assurance for delivering quality IT services. The Service Quality Plan provides the IT directorate with the tools needed to deliver what their customers want at the right time, at the right place and at the right price.

1.4   Target readership

This book is particularly relevant to managers involved in negotiating, reviewing and managing IT services and, more specifically, service levels. This book is also relevant to business managers to help them to establish IT services and support in terms of quality and quantity. Managers from supplier organisations may find this module relevant to setting up their own agreements with customers.

The target readership therefore includes the:

- IT Director
- IT management
- IT Services Manager
- IT Service Level Manager
- Business Information Manager
- Business Unit Managers
- Procurement Managers
- Supplier Managers
- Account Managers
- auditors.

1.5   Context

This book forms part of the IT Infrastructure Library. While it is of value read in isolation, its great benefit to an organisation comes from the broader understanding and application of IT service management techniques and functions. The interrelationships between the various IT service management functions are reflected in the integrated nature of the ITIL books. Readers are recommended therefore to read the ITIL books as elements of a whole and to implement their guidance holistically. This integration is especially evident when looking at service level management, as it depends directly upon the support of many other IT service management functions. The relationships between these functions are described in further detail in Chapter 2.

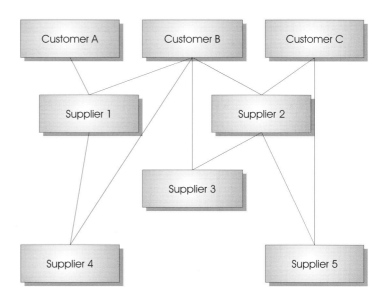

Figure 2: a complex interrelationship

In the real world we are all suppliers and customers, and this results in a complex interrelationship of delivered and supporting services. An agreement may be viewed from one perspective as an SLA and that same agreement for services may be seen from elsewhere as a supporting service; in some cases organisations will be supporting each other for different elements of the same service. For example, the IT applications development unit within an organisation will look to the IT services unit for the supply of on-line services while at the same time it may be supplying the underpinning software maintenance for those services. Naturally, in this book we occupy ourselves with good service level management practice, taking a simple, linear view of SLAs and underpinning services. It must always be borne in mind though, applying guidance to the, necessarily complicated, real world requires work in adapting to the circumstances, the company practice and the sheer scale and complexity that is to be found.

1.6   Related guidance

The IT Infrastructure Library (ITIL) has been written as part of an integrated set of guidance, each book addressing some aspect of IT service management. Some books, of which this is one, describe best practice for a specific IT service management function, while others address more general IT service management issues, such as planning and organisation, or offer complementary guidance.

A number of IT Infrastructure Library books are particularly relevant and are listed in the Bibliography.

1.7   Benefits, costs and possible problems

Effective service level management will deliver improvements in business performance and in customer perception of the delivered IT services, accompanied by an associated reduction in the impact on the business of poor service. IT services organisations themselves will benefit from the most structured approach possible to their delivery of IT services, from knowing what is expected of them and the improved planning, scheduling and budgeting that this allows. Although these kinds of benefits are complex to determine in advance, they can lead to large savings, improvements in staff morale and customer attitudes to IT. Internal or external benchmarking processes will best demonstrate the measurement of this improvement. These savings are likely to outweigh significantly the associated costs of implementing and running service level management.

To encourage management commitment, it is recommended that a short cost/benefit analysis takes place before starting the planning of the service level management process, comparing current costs and levels of customer satisfaction to what might be achievable. If possible it is recommended that both the IT services organisation and the customer organisations take a sponsorship in the service level management process, on the basis that both parties stand to benefit from high quality IT services.

When analysing the costs and benefits consider the following:

- existing service levels (number of current service breaks, time needed to restore services, response times, delivery times, service hours etc)

- the costs of non-compliance to the business (eg costs of down times)
  - missed business opportunities
  - unproductive staff times

- The costs to the IT services organisation of non-compliance with service levels
    - repair, replacement and reconstruction costs
    - IT staff time to record failures and restorative actions
    - use of alternative or additional means of delivering, communicating and recording work elements

- profile and image of the IT services organisation

- estimated improvements (calculated in user productivity)

- balance of benefits against costs (people, tools etc)

- net savings that may be achieved.

Also take into account those benefits that are more difficult to measure, such as improved user morale and satisfaction.

Agreements and clarification of IT services and service levels are vital in establishing a professional relationship between the IT services organisation and the customer organisation.

Other benefits from formalising the service level management process are:

- the Service Level Manager is responsible for achieving default, specific and consistent standards of service which can be measured, providing the customer's managers adhere to their side of the agreements

- the organisation is able to balance the levels of service required against the costs involved, and where customers are charged for the provision of IT services, the business unit is able to make this balance

- the ability to specify IT services brings long-term cost benefits by specifying the service components and resources required

- service improvement programmes lead to improved service quality giving increased user productivity

- the creation of a Service Quality Plan leads to a more effective and efficient service delivery and enables the IT management to maintain agreed service levels

- disputes on service delivery are resolved more quickly because of specifying service levels and delivery achievements in management reports

- IT services become more predictable, which builds user confidence and hence facilitates better utilisation by the business of the delivered IT services.

The costs associated with the implementation and running of the service level management process are roughly categorised as:

- staff costs (project team for implementation, Service Level Manager)

- training costs (including ITIL awareness, training in specific software tools, business awareness)

- documentation costs

- accommodation, hardware, software and other direct staff support costs

- maintaining the Service Catalogue, SLAs and the Service Quality Plan may lead to extra pressure on the operational activities.

The possible problems are summarised as follows:

- service level management expects or creates a professional relationship between the IT services organisation and the customer. This means that all employees of the IT services organisation are expected to maintain a professional attitude. The IT services organisation becomes a facilitator to the business – this often requires a change of attitude and culture which may be difficult for employees to accept

- the customer may need help to specify service requirements – this will require a level of support from IT specialists which should be regarded as a normal responsibility

- IT services and service levels must be specified with costs – the specification of service components might prove to be difficult. Effective negotiating techniques help to build acceptable specifications

- the Service Level Manager must guard against being over ambitious in agreeing service improvement targets before the necessary planning, monitoring and reporting tools, underlying procedures, Service Quality Plans and underpinning contracts are in place. A strategy of gradual improvement with regular checkpoints is recommended

- the overheads involved in actually monitoring and reporting on service level achievements can easily be underestimated. In large organisations this alone can be a full time job for several staff

- in practice IT service organisations often start with filling in SLAs to implement the service level management process for immediate benefits. However, starting with the SLAs means discarding vital process issues, such as making measurable agreements, being able to control the service achievements and defining the Service Quality Plan. This can result in a process which is difficult to manage and often in non-compliance with the actual required and delivered services and service levels. Annex D provides a project plan that can be used for implementing and running a successful service level management process.

2 The service level management process

2.1	**Introduction**	Businesses of all kind are becoming increasingly dependent on their IT to function. For many, survival for more than a day would be impossible without their IT services. As more and more business activities depend directly on the delivery of IT services, so business managers need to be aware of their IT requirements and to be confident that they have been specified and will be supplied by their IT provider.

This is equally true whether the IT services are provided in-house, by an external facilities management organisation or if there is a mix of supply.

2.2	**Goal**	Service level management is the process of negotiating, defining and managing the levels of IT service, that are required and cost justified.

This is, in turn, an integral part of the goal of IT service management: the delivery of a cost effective IT service that is of known quality, is quantity-based and meets or exceeds the customer's expectation.

2.3	**Results**	When defining a goal for service level management it is important to state clearly, and if possible quantify, the results that the service level management process should deliver. Examples of quantified results are:

- IT services are catalogued

- IT services are quantified in terms that both customer and IT provider understand

- internal and external targets of IT services are defined and agreed

- achievement of agreed service targets.

2.4	**Scope**	The scope of the service level management process concerns the management of IT services between:

- the customer organisation and the IT services organisation
    - default IT services and levels are defined in the Service Catalogue
    - the specific delivered IT services for a customer organisation are negotiated and defined in an SLA

- the IT services organisation and its external suppliers
  - agreed IT services have to be guaranteed by contracts with external suppliers
  - the agreements with external suppliers are defined in underpinning contracts

- the IT services organisation and its internal departments
  - agreed IT services lead to internal quantity and quality parameters
  - these parameters are defined in a Service Quality Plan
  - internal agreements covering this supply of service are known as operational level agreements (OLAs).

Figure 2 gives an outline of the scope of the service level management process.

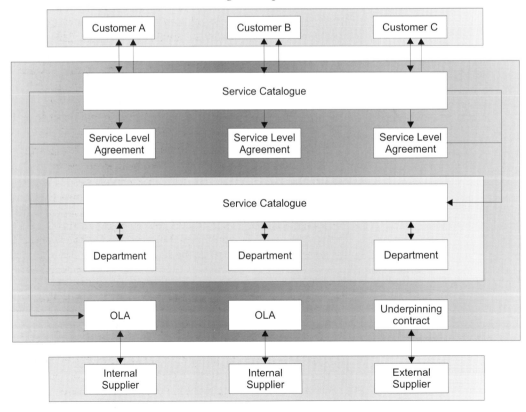

Figure 2: The scope of the service level management process

2.5 Activities

The Business can be defined here as that part of the organisation that uses the IT. The 'business' that is being undertaken does not necessarily have to be related in any way to IT.

The introduction of service level management should be a joint initiative by the IT services organisation and the business customer. The prime motivation should come from the business organisation; if it does not, the awareness campaign phase will prove to be the most crucial. It is essential that all parties involved, including IT services personnel, senior management and the user community, are made aware of why SLM is being introduced, what the benefits will be, how they will be affected, and what will be required of them.

The organisation's senior executive and business managers must be aware of service level management and its implications. They should pay particular attention to quality (the effect that poor service quality has on the efficient and effective running of the business or the costs of poor quality) and cost (a long-term cost saving is likely in most cases).

An awareness campaign to achieve the necessary managerial and financial commitment will be necessary when introducing service level management. This might take many forms including circulars, discussion papers, seminars and intranet. The awareness campaign should commence at the earliest possible stage, and must be targeted at both customer and IT staff. The need to maintain awareness and support among staff should not be viewed as a one-off task. However successful the initial awareness campaign has been, without ongoing effort customer and IT awareness will wane, with detrimental results. An approach to awareness campaigns is addressed in some detail in Annex F.

> For an awareness campaign to be truly effective a project sponsor should be appointed. It is to this that Europe's second largest company attributes the success of their quality improvement program. For each process to be implemented, a senior manager was appointed to monitor results and demonstrate the commitment of the business organisation.

In organisations where Total Quality Management (TQM) has been introduced, or business processes are managed according to quality assurance standards such as BS5750 or ISO9000, a successful introduction of service level management is very likely. In these organisations staff are accustomed to evaluating services in measurable units. In fact the ability to quantify services (both IT and non-IT) is an absolute prerequisite for obtaining a certificate for either case.

The activities in the process vary according to the respective stages of planning and implementing the process, using the process, and controlling the process. The stages represent the quality cycle for continuous improvement of the service level management process. The activities in all phases, however, are directed towards the defined goal.

Figure 3 shows the global overview of the service level management process.

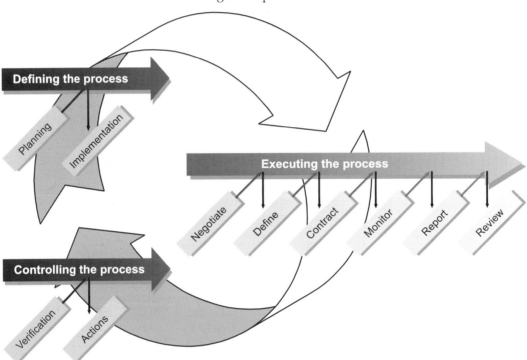

Figure 3: an overview of the SLM process

2.5.1   Defining the process

Introducing service level management into an organisation involves, by definition, resource commitment from different departments within the organisation, combined with at least confirmation and often re-negotiation of supporting services from within and without the organisation. To achieve this implementation in a timely and effective manner it is necessary to treat the introduction of SLM as a project. This is equally true when re-examining, reconstructing or redesigning an existing SLM structure. Transforming the SLM function, from one built upon packaging the delivered services, into a truly customer focused unit, transforming the infrastructure and attitudes to deliver services in the way the business needs, requires the structured and organised approach consistent with good project management.

Defining the process addresses the implementation of the process as well as adjustments later in the process.

An 'owner' for the process, responsible for the planning and implementation of the service level management process should be appointed. This may be the Service Level Manager, or may be a more senior individual (perhaps the IT Services Manager or IT Director).

2.5.2   Planning the process

The planning phase addresses the design of the SLM process and results in the delivery of an implementation plan. This plan should deliver the following:

- the appointment of the Service Level Manager(s) and supporting staff

- the service level management mission statement

- the scope of the services and the service level management process within the IT services organisation

- the awareness campaign (producing the communication plan – see Annex F)

- the definition of roles, tasks and responsibilities

- the quantification of the activities, time, money, people and quality needed

- the identification of the risks involved

- the assessment of the customer agreements structure and contracting issues

- the structure of SLAs, eg a three level hierarchy

- stages, responsibilities and target timetables

- documentation of customer organisations and suppliers

- documentation of relationships with other processes

- model Service Catalogue, SLA and Service Quality Plan

- agreed and accepted quality parameters

- contingency agreements

- the required support tools

- review of existing underpinning contracts and OLAs.

2.5.3 Implementing service level management

This phase comprises the execution of the plans prepared during the planning phase. The phase is closed with an evaluation of the planning and implementation phases. This evaluation will address both the suitability of the plan itself and its execution, including establishing the current awareness levels within the customer and IT services organisation.

The first step after appointing the Service Level Manager is to start the motivation phase of the awareness campaign.

Results of the implementation phase are:

- the appointment of the Service Level Manager

- the start of the awareness campaign (initiation and motivation phase)

- a Service Catalogue with existing services, default levels etc

- a model SLA (it is recommended that the implementation phase leads to a pilot SLA for one customer organisation. This is regarded as the first effective result that can be used for awareness issues)

- the initial Service Quality Plan is defined and agreed with internal service providers

- initial underpinning contracts are defined and agreed with suppliers

- supporting tools are implemented and running

- reviews of underpinning contracts are complete and supporting the agreed service levels

- procedures for the ongoing activities (negotiate, define, contract, review, report) are established.

2.5.4 Stages of implementing service level management

This section is concerned with the stages of implementing service level management and the actions and deliverables associated with each stage. Deliverables include a Service Catalogue, SLAs, underpinning contracts and a Service Quality Plan. Guidance on defining the contents of these products can be found in Chapter 3 *Quantifying IT services*.

Negotiate

The key to successful service level management is to ensure that the function remains focused on the customer throughout planning, implementation and ongoing management. This means that the customer's views are the defining force for IT services. Principally, it is the shape and nature of the customer's organisation that shapes the SLAs. The targets against which the delivered IT services will be measured are those of the customer, not those of the IT supplier.

A customer-focused organisation requires integration of the marketing function with the operational activities. Information gathered from the operational activities provides an understanding of the customer's actual behaviour. Information gathered from other sources, such as written or telephone enquiries, interviews and third party market research provides evidence of the customers attitudes, perceptions, wishes and expectations. At least as important as all of these is the direct day-to-day contact between IT supplier and customer, which takes place at several levels between the two units.

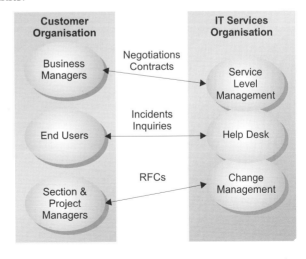

Figure 5: Organisational levels

Figure 5 is an example of the organisational levels of customer contact described in ITIL.

Service level requirements are negotiated and agreed with business managers. Section or Project Managers often request changes in the agreed IT services delivery. End-users of services contact the help desk with incidents and enquiries.

The information that can be gathered via these proven channels is inherently practical, reflecting the operational needs of the organisation's day-to-day business. They offer the key to moving the organisation from a 'product-out' to a 'market-in' focus.

The first step in coming to an agreement about the delivered IT services, is to define an authorisation structure (who signs what). A structure is needed that reflects the services required by the customer and the way the customer organisation is structured. Specifically, it should not be built upon the way the services are administered, designed, maintained or supported within the IT services organisation.

Figure 6 shows a typical SLA configuration that defines the authorisation structure with a customer.

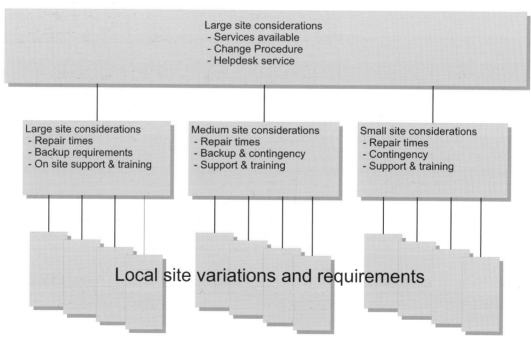

Figure 6: Typical SLA structure

In this example the Service Catalogue describes the IT services at a corporate level. The service levels in the Service Catalogue apply to all customers. The SLA at customer level applies to all the selected services for one customer group. The SLA at service level applies to one specific service for a specific customer group.

> The IT services organisation within a tax services organisation defined a Service Catalogue at corporate level. This Service Catalogue defined all the default IT services that could be provided.
>
> At the level of the separate tax services (eg customs, income taxes, road taxes) a master SLA was defined. The master SLA defined the default service levels for every section within that particular tax service.
>
> For the separate sections within the services individual SLAs were defined. Each SLA defined the service levels applicable to individual working groups within the section concerned.

> The IT services organisation within a clearing house defined a Service Catalogue for all customer organisations with service levels for default availability, transaction times, line capacity, quantities, delivery times and possible connections.
>
> For every customer organisation the specific availability, transaction times, line capacity, quantities, delivery times, connections and connection lines were defined in one SLA.

Define

SLR – expressed by the customer. Commonly this will be an element in the specification and development of a new service but is equally relevant when revisiting existing service levels.

The service level requirements (SLR) must be clearly defined and agreed on. Service requirements can be regarded as demands on the service provider – they form one of the initial inputs to the negotiation procedures that will result in agreed SLAs. The activities needed to define the service requirements are described in Chapter 3, *Quantifying IT services*.

Contract

The service specifications are defined in the Service Catalogue (for default IT services and corporate level IT services) and in SLAs (for specific IT services and for customer and service level IT services).

The activities needed to define the service requirements; Service Catalogue, SLAs, Service Quality Plan and underpinning contracts are described in Chapter 3 *Quantifying IT services*.

Monitor

To monitor the service level management process the IT service achievements have to be clearly defined. Service achievements are the delivered service levels within a defined time-span.

The service achievements have to meet the agreed external targets. These must be monitored from the customer's perspective. The ability to use the IT services does not depend merely on technical issues. Information and knowledge are essential prerequisites for using services. The definitions of external and internal targets are discussed in Chapter 3 *Quantifying IT Services.*

> A user complained to the help desk that he had been unable to use his IT services at all during the day. IT had recorded the system as being unavailable for 2 hours only – why did he feel it had been unavailable all day?
>
> Further investigation showed that the user, having reported the mainframe failure, had shut down his PC, expecting to be informed when the system was available again. The next day he logged on in the morning as usual and the system worked – no-one had thought to inform him the day before, when the system had become available, and he had no reason to leave his PC running when the mainframe service he required was not available to him, and had thus not received automatic messages across the network.

Internal targets are normally monitored, often automatically, within availability management and capacity management, and for some aspects of the service within the processes used to manage calls, incidents and problems. Measuring of system parameters that relate to IT's internal processes is important, but of course is not sufficient. It is important that measures relate to the customer's perception of the delivered service and so escalation times, delivery times, support services etc have to be monitored too. This means that metrics have to be introduced within processes such as help desk and change management. The management information for systems as well as service management has to be combined to give a complete overview of service achievements.

Report

Management reports must be generated on a regular basis. The reports are distributed on the basis of need or request. The contents of the reports generated will depend on the reader, eg Business Manager, process owner, Service Level Manager.

Management reports typically show service achievements measured against agreed external targets. Examples of service achievements are:

- availability over a measured period and measured unavailability (eg downtime)

- average peak-hour response times

- number of functional errors in each IT service

- frequency and duration of any system operating below acceptable level

- average number of users during peak-hours

- peak-hour transaction rates

- attempted security violations.

Management reports might also contain metrics showing current levels and trends over time including:

- number of SLAs in place

- number of breaches of SLAs

- costs of monitoring and reporting on SLAs

- customer satisfaction – through surveys, registered complaints etc

- call, incident, problem and change statistics.

Review

Service levels are reviewed on a regular basis. Reviewing service achievements is the responsibility of the Service Level Manager. During such a review, typically the following issues would be discussed:

- service achievements since last meeting

- service related problems

- identification of service trends

- changes to the service that take place within the agreed levels in the SLA (the change management function must be involved)

- the initiation of any procedural changes (such as re-scheduling workloads, demand management or tuning) or the preparation of any financial cases required for additional resources

- non-compliance (penalties, corrective actions etc).

If service levels are not met the Service Level Manager and customer will discuss the options available to improve matters, these might include:

- service improvement programmes

- commitment of extra resources, staff and/or equipment and, crucially, how these extra resources might be funded

- readjustment of targets

- reduction in throughput

- alternative working practices.

Operational level achievements are reviewed with the appropriate internal operational managers. If the agreements in the Service Quality Plan are not met, corrective action must be taken. In general this means that the operational tasks must be changed and may require more resources (human and/or technical). Typically, the review of internal requirements is undertaken as part of availability management, help desk and problem management.

Underpinning contracts must be reviewed regularly with the supplier managers to ensure that they continue to support the agreements with customers. The review of the underpinning contracts is similar to the review of the Service Catalogue and the SLAs, with the Service Level Manager representing the customer organisation and the supplier manager representing the service provider.

2.5.5   Controlling the process

For organisations to improve their performance it is essential to review achieved results against the original goals. These controls do not relate to the achievement of service levels, but to the extent in which the IT services organisation has succeeded in designing their services and internal targets according to the customer's requirements.

Control takes place by taking actions on signals (reactive) and proactive analysis concerning the process execution.

Proactive control anticipates future problems and deficiencies by:

- forecasting changes in service requirements or capacity

- analysing requests for change (RFCs) affecting the IT services

- being aware of the impact of technology, environmental and broader business change

- initiating corrective action to prevent any detrimental effect before it is noticed by the customer, or in practice before it breaches agreed service levels.

*Reactiv*e control takes action concerning:

- problems found within the service level management process

- deficiencies signalled from the help desk, problem management, change management, availability management, capacity management and contingency planning

- deficiencies signalled from management reports and audits

- requests for change within the change management process.

2.5.6   Verification, quality assurance and audit

The service level management process must be reviewed regularly for effectiveness. The procedures must be verified against the way of working and the current needs of the organisation and its customers. This review will normally be carried out twice yearly.

The organisation is likely to have a policy on the auditing of internal functions that will apply equally to the service level management function. An audit may be carried out by external auditors, an internal audit unit or by staff from a different operational area within the organisation. Such an audit will be carried out by staff independent of the function. Internal quality assurance work will also examine the adherence to laid down procedures within the service level management process.

Typically, regular auditing might take place annually and also on an *ad hoc* basis (at the request of the process owner or other stakeholders). *Ad hoc* audits may restrict their focus to particular aspects of the process.

Assessable aspects include:

- consistency of the Service Catalogue and the SLAs with the service achievements, Service Quality Plan and underpinning contracts

- existence of authorised Service Catalogue, SLAs, Service Quality Plan and underpinning contracts

- effectiveness and efficiency of the process, procedures and instructions

- consistency of the procedures and instructions with the ongoing situation

- formal review of the quantity and quality of the IT services.

It is the responsibility of the assessor to analyse the results and signal problems and areas for improvement and identify non-conformance to be addressed. It is the responsibility of the process owner to take action on these results. A timeframe to correct non-conformance should be agreed and a follow-up review scheduled to confirm action completion.

2.6 Relationships

This section describes the relationships between service level management and other processes. Several reports and activities, needed for optimal service level management, are delivered or executed within other processes.

The Service Level Manager must take care not to sign-up to over ambitious SLAs too early. It is preferable to take a cautious position initially, with room for improvement as service targets are achieved. The SLA can be reviewed or changed by either party at a mutually agreed date. The SLA should be a 'living' document.

For formal service level management a number of supporting processes need to be established. It is essential that processes be well organised for the following:

- availability management

- capacity management

- incident and problem management

- change management.

Depending on the priorities and business environment of the organisation, other, different, supporting processes will be considered essential. For example:

- business continuity management – in most countries government legislation requires financial organisations to have acceptable continuity planning

- security – in defence organisations obviously, but also to protect many organisation's long-term strategy and marketing planning

- cost management – where internal 'hard charging' has been adopted.

A brief overview of these processes and their relationships with the service level management process is provided in the following sections.

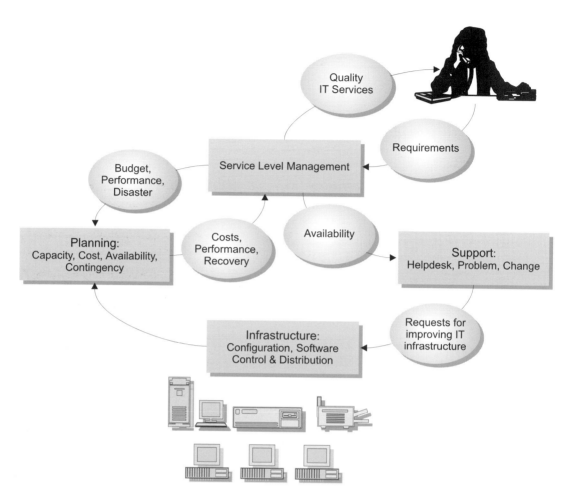

Figure 7: Relationships

2.6.1 Availability
management

The Availability Manager has overall responsibility for
the availability of all services running. This may include
the responsibility of negotiating and managing the
underpinning contracts with suppliers. Large
organisations will typically have a separate procurement
function.

Availability management is responsible for the delivery
of service achievement reports (availability statistics).
Analysis has to be made by reviewing the achievements
against the agreed service levels. Availability
management supports the monitoring activity.

The availability management function should also be
responsible, working with capacity management, for
calculating and modelling achievable and affordable

availability levels in new and revised IT services. The results of this work will be a major input to initial discussions for SLAs relating to new or changed services.

2.6.2 Capacity management

Capacity management is responsible for the delivery of the capacity plan. This plan needs to review the current installed hardware and software, what the current usage is, what the developments are in the capacity usage and the customers needs and how the IT services organisation can adhere to the total amount of expected usage.

Activities concerning tuning, upgrades and changes have to be agreed with the Service Level Manager. Capacity management reports to the Service Level Manager about the capacity plan and advises the Service Level Manager concerning demand management.

Capacity management delivers reports for performance, resource and workload management. Capacity management supports the monitoring and defining activities.

In particular the capacity management process provides the Service Level Manager with information about the customers' needs (the capacity plan) and changing IT services for the coming period. Also capacity management designs the IT infrastructure services according to agreed services and service levels and delivers performance reports.

2.6.3 Incident and problem management

The entire incident reporting and resolution process is essential to the delivery of a quality IT service. This is supported by the help desk and problem management functions explained in more detail below.

Help desk

The help desk is the day-to-day contact between the users and the IT services organisation. Users should be encouraged to contact the help desk about any service enquiries or deficiencies in service quality. The help desk service levels, the service hours and the ways to contact the help desk should be incorporated into the Service Catalogue and SLAs.

Escalation procedures are discussed between the Service Level Manager and the Business Manager. The help desk is then responsible for the registration of incident details and statistics. If, due to incidents, the service levels are expected to be endangered the help desk must inform service level management.

The help desk is able to monitor and report, both to the service level management function and to business customers, on many aspects of service achievement.

Problem management

Escalation procedures are discussed and agreed between the Service Level Manager and the Business Manager. Problem management is then responsible for the registration of problem details and statistics. If, due to problems, the service levels are expected to be endangered the Problem Manager needs to inform the Service Level Manager and to implement the procedures according to the agreement.

2.6.4 Change management

Any change to existing IT services or IT infrastructure could have implications on service achievements. Change management verifies requests for change against the Service Catalogue and SLAs. SLAs may include targets for implementing and commenting on changes within agreed deadlines, depending upon priorities or impact. Escalation times and change workflow are discussed between the Service Level Manager and the Business Manager.

2.6.5 Contingency planning

Contingency planning is responsible for the continuity of the IT service provision by reducing the impact of major incidents, emergencies or disasters. Contingency planning reports to the Service Level Manager concerning contingency plans and test results.

It is recommended that contingency planning for the delivery of IT services is part of the SLA. It is essential for the business that IT services can quickly be recovered and delivered to the agreed quality even if disaster strikes the IT Infrastructure. This function is also an integral part of the organisation's business continuity management, which should have plans designed to protect all aspects of the organisation's business, not just IT provision. The Service Level Manager therefore needs to work with any existing business continuity management (BCM) plans and with those devising and maintaining them.

2.6.6 Security management

Security management is responsible for the security of the offered IT services. Attempted security violations must be reported to the Service Level Manager. Security requirements may well impose constraints on the service level management process including:

- restricted access to business information

- system access security requirements that preclude a homogenous organisation-wide approach

- physical security requirements that restrict maintenance and support access to some users and equipment

- allocation of particular staff (ie security cleared or local citizens) to specific customer areas.

2.6.7 Configuration management

Configuration management is responsible for the registration of all components of the IT services. Configuration management registers the Service Catalogue, SLAs, underpinning contracts, Service Quality Plan, customer organisations and suppliers.

2.6.8 Cost management

Cost management registers and maintains the users and cost accounts concerning the usage of components in the IT infrastructure. Cost management supplies statistics and reports. Cost aspects that are to be involved in the Service Catalogue and SLAs are agreed between the Cost Manager and the Service Level Manager.

2.6.9 Customer liaison

The customer liaison function can be implemented as an interface for liaison between the customer organisation and the IT services organisation. Demand management then is the responsibility of the customer liaison function.

2.6.10 Applications development and software maintenance

It would be difficult to over-emphasise the benefits that can accrue to an organisation by considering service management aspects of new or revised software at the design stage. The service level management function must be in the vanguard of this process. As the professionals, the SLM staff should be working with the customers to determine agreed service levels that reflect customer need and value for money in terms of the ongoing cost of providing and maintaining those service levels.

Once the target service levels have been established, the information will be a vital source of input to applications design, capacity management, availability management, contingency planning and many other functions. Those involved in these areas will find their jobs easier and the cost of errors smaller by becoming involved at an early stage, and most especially before the service has been built and delivered.

2.7 Roles and responsibilities

Processes tend to span the organisation's hierarchy. Therefore it is very important to define the responsibilities associated with the activities in the process that have to be performed. To remain flexible it is advisable to use the concept of roles. A role is defined as a set of responsibilities, tasks and authorisations. In this chapter, very brief examples of relevant roles within the service level management process are defined. In addition the contribution of established hierarchical functions (eg the IT director) to the process is briefly outlined. Roles must be assigned to people or groups within the organisation. The roles, their interaction and responsibilities are described and discussed in further detail both in the ITIL books addressing the appropriate functions and in more generally targeted ITIL books including *IT Services Organisation* and *ITIL practices in small IT units*.

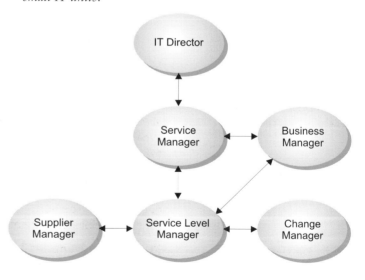

Figure 8: Interactions

2.7.1	IT Director	Within the service level management process the IT Director is typically responsible for the official signature of the Service Catalogue, SLAs and underpinning contracts. The IT Director must take an active role in the awareness campaign and the commitment for the Service Quality Plan.
2.7.2	IT Services Manager	The IT Services Manager is responsible for all the service management processes within the IT services organisation. The IT Services Manager is responsible for quality assurance of the function.
2.7.3	Service Level Manager	The Service Level Manager, being the process owner, naturally performs a key role in the service level management process. The responsibilities of the Service Level Manager are:

- to develop and maintain the Service Catalogue

- to perform the activities as described within the execution of the process (negotiate, define, contract, monitor, review, report)

- to analyse and review the agreed service levels

- to report service achievements

- to initiate service improvement programmes

- to co-ordinate audits and management reports.

Guidance and an example of clauses appropriate to an SLM role description can be found in Annex D.

2.7.4	Business Manager	Service levels are negotiated with the Business Manager as the responsible function within the customer's organisation. The Business Manager is responsible for the official signature of the SLA.
2.7.5	Supplier Manager	Underpinning contracts are negotiated with the Supplier Manager as the responsible function within the supplier organisation. The Supplier Manager will be responsible for the official signature of underpinning contracts.
2.7.6	Change Manager	Requests for change will have potential impact on service levels. The Change Manager is responsible for ensuring that impacts are identified, costed and considered in the change management process.

2.7.7 Section managers

Operational level requirements are discussed and agreed with the appropriate section head supplying the service. Essential supporting services are likely to cover wide areas of the organisation, not just the IT directorate, some examples might be:

- Network Manager

- office services

- internal mail services

- personnel division

- software maintenance

- technical support.

3 Quantifying IT services

3.1 Why quantify IT services?

As the dependence of business organisations on their IT services has increased dramatically over time, the business demand for quality IT services has grown stronger. A quality service is a service that lives up to the expectations of the customer. The only possible way to deliver a quality service is by knowing what the customer wants. There is no exception to this!

To be of benefit in designing and monitoring the service level management process, the understanding of customer needs must be quantifiable. Unless some agreed method of quantifying the service is established with the customer, it is not possible to determine whether the IT services function is on course to achieve its targets.

The service level management process plays a key role in understanding and defining what customers want. This chapter shows how to define clearly the demands of IT customers and how to achieve proactive and controlled service delivery.

3.2 Approach

Quantifying IT services or defining the scope and level of service the customer wants is regarded here as a design process. According to the model for quality assurance in design, development, production, installation and servicing (ISO9001: 1994) the design process has to be controlled to assure that specified demands are met in the end product or service. In this chapter a method is developed for designing an IT service.

Figure 9: service design process

3.3   The customer

Experience shows that customers take certain aspects of a service for granted, they may therefore not state all their demands, since they implicitly expect them to be met. This makes it crucial that IT service management genuinely gets to know its customers.

The Quality Manager really needed some time off. He decided to check into a hotel for a nice, quiet evening away from the daily routine. Having some experience with first defining a quality service in order to expect it, he decided to clearly state his expectations in advance. These were:

- a single room with one bed
- a television set available
- a telephone
- shower and bath in the room
- room service.

When he checked in that evening everything was as promised earlier. However, he didn't perceive the service rendered as a quality service. The problem was that the bed in his room was only four feet long. The hotel claimed that he didn't specify the length of the bed, so who was to blame?

The SLA in which the attitude and behaviour of help desk personnel is specified will probably never be written. Internal IT services organisations should be aware of their advantage – that they truly know the art of the business, as well as the organisation culture and management style, of their customers. External providers would have to put in extra effort to compensate for their initial disadvantage.

These assumed items that traditionally have been left to 'common sense', rather than explicitly defined, are a constant source of confusion and conflict where a service has recently been outsourced. The customers expect the unstated items to be delivered as before, but if they are not mentioned in the contract, then there may be no obligation to deliver.

3.4   Defining service level requirements

The IT manager of a governmental institution sighed: "I can't believe this. All the effort I put into service management seems to go to waste. I've got all the necessary documents ready for signing. The department simply doesn't understand the advantages I am offering..."

The first step in quantifying new or existing IT services is to (re)define, on a general level, what the customer expects of the service. These expectations are defined as (user) service level requirements (SLRs).

It is very important at this stage that the user community is actively involved in stating these requirements. When this has been achieved, the battle for quality is half won.

At the beginning of this stage the Service Level Manager has to prepare for the discussion with the user community. The first question that needs to be addressed is: 'What is IT service and of what components does it consist?' A service may range from access to a single software application program, to the use of one or more global facilities (eg a transaction processing system or a global communications network).

The mapping of users on to particular services or their components must also be negotiated. The Service Level Manager must produce a plan giving proposals of how the users will be grouped together, the scope of each service, and who the signatories will be, as a basis for discussions with users.

When discussing service level requirements, the following aspects have to be specified and documented:

- customer demands

- an approximate description of customer requirements

- a description of the result for the customer in terms of functional requirements

- contribution to business performance in terms of
    - effectiveness (test against business policy)
    - efficiency (test against way of working)

- consequences in terms of
    - efforts for the IT directorate
    - expected additional investments

- instructions regarding the design of the service

- date from which the service must be available

- date when each design phase will be completed

- who will design the service

- what IT functions will be involved in delivering the service

- reference to the present way of working and/or quality standards that have to be taken into account when designing the service

- reference to the SLA that will be replaced if applicable

- indication of the possible service levels that could be provided.

The product of this phase is a document to be signed by the Service Level Manager on behalf of the IT directorate and a business manager. An example of this document is shown in Annex D.

As the service develops through the various stages of design, procurement and implementation, a number of system modifications may result in amendments to the agreed service requirements. This process will involve iterative consultations with the users and close liaison with the applications development function.

3.5   Specifying service levels

In the specification phase the service level requirements are worked out in great detail. The specification phase has the following goals:

- an unambiguous and detailed description of an IT service and its components

- specification of the manner in which the service is to be delivered to assure that agreed targets can and will be met

- specification of the demands on quality control of delivered services in order to be able to constantly meet the specified demands, thereby achieving customer satisfaction.

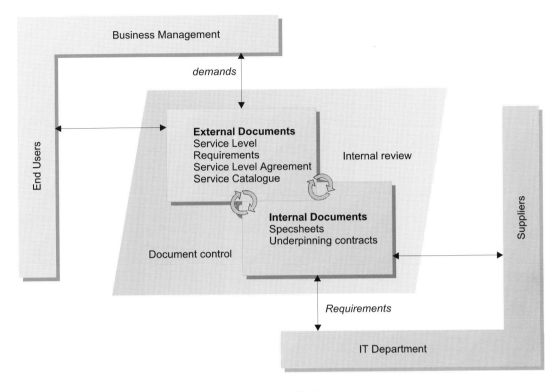

Figure 10: The specification phase

In the specification phase it is advisable to separate documents for internal use from documents for external use. Documents for external use refer to targets that are agreed with the customer; it is these targets that drive the process. These documents have to be developed in close collaboration with the user community and will be become the input for the documents for internal use.

> 'I like to compare my IT directorate with the water company. Everybody depends on the fact that fresh water runs from the tap on request. But nobody really cares how the water company's organisation is structured, or of what components their technical infrastructure consists to achieve this daily miracle'
>
> *The former IT Exploitation Manager of a European insurance company*

Documents for internal use refer to targets within the IT organisation which have to be met in order meet agreed customer requirements. Following the 'water company' metaphor; these documents will be produced within the IT services organisation.

A division between the parts of the document for external and internal use can be of tremendous help when the service level management process is up and running. The management of service levels thereafter is just a matter of keeping both parts of the document in harmony. The instruments for achieving this balance (internal review and document control) are discussed in this chapter. Another advantage is that the IT directorate doesn't need to bother its customers with technical specifications. This enables an SLA to be produced that is comprehensive for both IT and business staff.

The use of specification sheets (specsheets) can usefully play a major role in the process of designing SLAs.

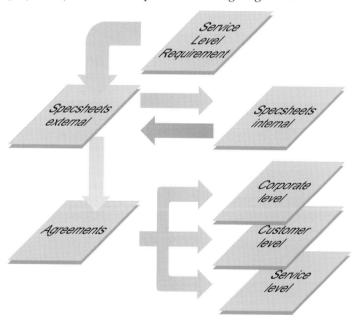

Figure 11:Specsheets

The purpose of a specsheet is to specify in detail what the customer wants (external) and what consequences this has for the service provider (internal) such as required resources or skills. Specsheets do not require signatories and should be placed under document control.

The formal SLA and/or Service Catalogue can be built directly from the specsheets. As a consequence, when changes to service levels are made, the specsheets are always altered. Consequently the SLA is rebuilt from the changed specsheet. By adopting this practice, the service provider can, under all circumstances, guarantee that the agreed internal quality targets are in line with external demands. The delivery of quality (IT) services is, therefore, shown to be supported adequately.

> An example of a very effective document control procedure.
>
> When reference is made to certain external documents not part of the service design (for instance user or system documentation) a list of these external documents should be produced. On this list all documents related to the particular service are listed, including:
>
> - their version number and date of issue
>
> - the location where the original document is kept
>
> - a recipient or distribution list for each document
>
> - how updates to these documents are brought to the attention of the designer of the service so that all possible consequences of these changes for service levels can be taken under consideration.

Specsheets should be constructed for internal as well as for external use. In the following paragraphs the various specsheets are discussed. In Annex D, an overview of an example specsheet is supplied.

3.5.1 Specsheet service external

The specsheet service external contains information concerning customer demands. In this document customer demands are quantified as measurable targets. Also responsibilities for the delivery and the assurance of the quality service are defined. When gathering the information, the service level requirement document drives the process. Where certain aspects need further clarification, the user community should be involved. The following information should be provided.

General

Name of the service
Use names that are familiar throughout the organisation; beware of assuming that all parts of an organisation understand the same jargon.

Description of service component functionality

The results of the service should be defined in a way that allows customers to verify if the service is indeed delivered as agreed. All SLAs must further include some agreed minimum level of acceptable functional requirement. Regardless of how rigorous quality assurance and testing procedures are, no significant IT system will ever be completely error free. Whenever errors are detected it is important to assess the severity in order to decide what priority and resources, if any, should be allocated to resolving the problem.

An IT service exists to support the customer's business operation, and therefore assessments of the severity must be derived from the impact of the error on that business operation. Traditionally however, severity scales have been expressed in the terms of the IT supplier, often more related to the type of hardware affected than the type of business operation inconvenienced, or perhaps crippled, by the error. Nonetheless, some example of typical errors for each severity level is an essential aid to using the system in practice. Some general rules for severity scales can be useful:

- keep the number of categories as small as possible; the human mind is rarely comfortable with more than three options, especially when a quick categorisation is required; (this approach, in battlefield triage, has stood for some 3000 years as best practice)

- use examples that will be understandable to all customers and IT services

- be certain that responsibility for allocating and agreeing the severity is clear and widely known

- in the absence of alternatives, try to express the consequences in financial terms to the organisation's business

- do not be frightened of using simple terms for describing the priority levels eg:
    1. can't do something important
    2. please fix it as soon as you can but I can get on with something else now
    3. I can live without it for a while.

All fault-reporting mechanisms must include provision for severity levels to be recorded, and these must be monitored, and comparisons must be made with the SLAs. The subject is addressed in more detail in ITIL as part of *Incident and Problem Management*.

The duration of the service
This refers to the time period in which the agreement is valid. It is common to specify a period of one year, which is automatically extended for another year if neither party requests a re-negotiation.

The location of the service; where is it to be delivered?
In geographically dispersed environments it is necessary to provide location specific details of the provided service. To what location is the service to be delivered and, from what location is the service to be delivered? This also indicates the level of support that can be expected.

Required initial investments to deliver the service
This information is derived in conjunction with the Cost Manager, refer to the ITIL cost management book.

IT staff time to deliver the service
A careful estimation of the hours required, both for one-off and ongoing efforts will, where a new service is provided, lead to improved determination of the staff requirements within the IT directorate. When accurately made it provides IT management with helpful information concerning the appropriate and justified staffing levels.

Information, products and facilities to be supplied by the customer
In many companies the user community literally owns IT hardware or software resources, especially in the end-user environment. It is critical that there is a clear understanding of where the responsibility for the availability of IT resources lies within the IT directorate.

In other cases the service can only be delivered if the customer provides certain information or facilities. This should be specified clearly, as this is what a user needs to know in advance in order to be prepared when asking for a particular service. An example is the information that is typically needed when asking for a user-id.

Aftercare

This applies to a form of guarantee on delivered products or services and describes to what extent aftercare can be expected.

General terms of delivery

Depending on the relationship with the customer a reference can be made to a more formal document in which the general delivery terms are specified.

Service levels

Quality or acceptance criteria

These acceptance criteria, against which the customer can accept the service as delivered, form the heart of the SLA. Criteria have to be very carefully defined in quantifiable and understandable units. This is especially necessary in the modern distributed environments. The definition of availability for instance is very tricky. Availability can be defined on 'server' or on 'client' level. Of course, the user organisation will, all other things being equal, prefer a criterion set on client or end-user level. However the level of information reflects directly on the associated management cost. It is then the task of the service provider to produce a balance sheet of what degree of measurement can be done at what cost. In modern technology virtually everything is possible, the customer should make the decision on what level information must be supplied. The golden rule for the service provider remains: if you cannot or will not measure it, don't agree to it.

Another typical quality criterion is the reliability of a particular service. Reliability means freedom from failure. It is determined by the reliability of each part of the infrastructure, the resilience built into the IT service and the level of preventative maintenance. A way to measure reliability is the number of service failures or the number of jobs that have to be re-run due to error.

It is important that quality criteria are carefully defined and that all parties fully understand the consequences. Because the focus of this agreement is on the result for the customer and not on the efforts required to produce this result, quality criteria must, at the minimum, consist of the description of the result within a specified timeframe.

Criteria can be defined by specifying the following aspects:

- target – the target clearly specifies the agreement; for instance the network is available 98% of opening hours

- measurement criteria – defining the target in understandable and measurable units; for instance the network is available when any one user can communicate with any other user

- who measures and how, how is it recorded and by whom? It is important that the method of measurement of targets is agreed in advance. Answering this question also obliges the Service Level Manager to delegate responsibility for providing correct management information.

Timetables
- Time to service delivery – date or time from which the service can be delivered

- Service hours – the hours when the service can be delivered. In some cases this might be round the clock, seven days a week

- Waiting time – the time that might elapse between the request for the service and the moment of service delivery

- Processing time – the time it actually takes to provide the service. The processing time is by definition smaller or equal to waiting time

- Time to respond to, and to fix, incidents.

Security, backup and recovery and contingency planning
- Security – here the security measures related to the delivery of the service are specified. Security measures can vary from limiting physical access to the computer room to the use of user-ids and passwords

- Contingency – it is specified what measures the IT directorate has taken to be able to continue the service delivery if unexpected events or even disasters occur. Design a separate SLA for the contingency situation. Please refer to the related ITIL module on contingency planning for further details.

Quality, quantity and availability of IT personnel
- What personnel will be available during service hours

- What is their skill level, how many are required?

Agreed procedures

Procedures required for signing the SLA
These are the procedures laid down for agreeing the SLA, including: who signs the agreement, who is to be consulted, timescales etc.

Change procedures
An SLA is not a static document, but is under the influence of constant change. It is important to state that changes to the document will only be accepted if both parties agree on them.

Customer acceptance procedure
How the customer formally accepts the service delivered as agreed. It is quite common to define a procedure of silent acceptance, for instance if there are no complaints within a month the service is considered to be accepted.

Procedures or working instructions set by the customer
This paragraph leaves room for special conditions that are set or certain procedures that are agreed upon when delivering the service. In the specsheet for external use, only those steps in which the customer plays a role have to be defined. These procedures or conditions could for example be related to the use of a project management methodology that the customer prefers.

Procedures of service delivery
Define what sequential steps have to be taken to deliver the service. This paragraph often can be combined with the procedures or working instructions set by the customer.

Error reporting
It is very important that the IT directorate provides customers with an interface to communicate errors in services. This is described in the ITIL books covering incident and problem management. They also describe how the help desk handles the previously mentioned severity codes. The severity codes used at the help desk must relate to the SLA targets in order to produce meaningful measurements of SLA performance via the help desk. The provision of a help desk can also be regarded as a separate service. This mainly applies to a

help desk service with a business support function. In this paragraph the reporting procedure can be specified, including for instance a phone number or email address.

3.5.2 Specsheet service internal

The specsheet service internal contains all the information relating to the control, assembly and monitoring of the components that make up the IT services. The following describe typical contents.

Standards, legislation and policies
It is important to consider some general consequences of providing IT services. Of course, not all standards or legislation apply to all services. However, the exercise of filling in the blanks protects the Service Level Manager from unexpected restrictions at the time the service is fully designed and ready for delivery. The following standards or legislation might require reference:

- public health standards
- public safety standards
- environmental standards
- data protection and privacy legislation
- legal standards or legislation
- necessary insurance.

In addition to legislative requirements, there may well be business agreements and organisational policy that produce general consequences. One example might be the cut-off time for the receipt of orders in order to guarantee a same day service vital to the business marketing strategy.

Internal ongoing cost of providing the service
Depending on the level to which cost management is implemented in the IT organisation the internal cost of providing the service can be more or less accurately calculated. For organisations that do not intend to charge their customers for IT services, a reference to the IT budget can be made. Where charging for IT services is in operation, the invoice can often be associated with the SLA; in this way the customer associates the service provided directly with the charge – they can easily see what they are getting for their money. Equally the IT Services Manager and staff are reminded that this is a genuine customer-supplier relationship.

Delivery date
This reflects the date on which the IT directorate is ready to deliver the service according to the agreed service levels.

Delivery procedure
The delivery procedure consists of a number of sequential activities that have to be performed in order to deliver the required service. Make sure that this can be checked in a later stage, by for instance producing a checklist. A delivery procedure at the minimum consists of:

- (a representative of) the customer signs the contract with a reference to the specsheet

- IT staff are informed about the delivery start date and the service concerned

- the last step always encompasses a form of test or final check to assure that all previous steps are successfully completed.

Required additional procedures
Reference can be made to the standard operating procedures within the IT directorate. In the process of defining the service and especially when defining the delivery process, it should be considered if a standard way of working is required or that a set of guidelines will suffice. When a standard way of working is required, but not yet agreed upon, the procedure will have to be designed and approved.

Quality, quantity and availability of IT personnel
The required skills of IT personnel are identified. The need for extra training is evaluated or perhaps the (temporary) hiring of external staff is considered. The quantity of personnel associated with the delivery of the service is also estimated. This may have consequences for the staffing of the IT directorate, which can influence the cost associated to the service. Finally the required availability of IT personnel is defined. This could affect shift times, the introducing of pager services etc. Clearly these aspects have to be planned well in advance.

Internal targets

To provide a certain level of any IT services to customers, internal targets have to be set. Internal targets vary according to the nature of the external targets. Some internal targets have a technical nature, for instance the maximum extent to which the total network capacity can be used. Internal targets can also refer to the escalation times of incidents with certain predefined severity or impact codes. Internal targets have to be set in such a way that they guarantee compliance to the defined customer acceptance or quality criteria. Devise these targets in a similar way to the customer acceptance criteria.

Internal targets should be secured in the organisation via the service quality plan. In this plan corrective actions should also be specified. Corrective actions have to be undertaken if and when internal targets are not met, or better, when it is apparent that they will not be met. Furthermore planning for improving the internal targets should be addressed. Guidance on the Service Quality Plan is given in Chapter 4.

The monitoring of the service level management process will largely be concentrated on these internal targets. Figure 12 illustrates how regular internal reviews can verify whether internal targets are still in balance with the external targets. Customer satisfaction enquiries and the customer acceptance procedure help to verify whether external targets balance the customer requirements. Where inconsistencies are detected, the service must be redesigned to ensure that the entire process supports the business needs. The frequency of monitoring and reporting suggested in the figure is based on practice, representing an optimal balance between the efforts of producing information and the profits of using it. The frequency of monitoring should, of course, be matched to the circumstances faced by the IT services organisation.

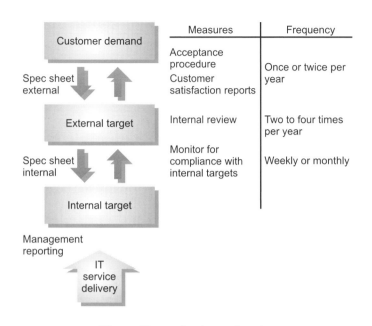

Figure 12: monitoring and review

External dependencies

If the IT directorate does not have control over all the components that determine the quality of the required service (and in most cases it does not) this should be clearly stated. Furthermore an action plan of how these dependencies are dealt with should be devised. Dealing with external dependencies means minimising the impact of these dependencies on the agreed level of service. Common external dependencies are utility companies that provide electricity and external cable and telecommunications suppliers.

External dependencies can be dealt with by the use of underpinning contracts. By carefully reviewing the contents of the contracts with suppliers and maintainers of IT infrastructure components, the IT directorate can ensure that these contracts continue to support the users' requirements. Where the review shows that a contract does not fully meet requirements, or cannot continue to meet requirements for the duration of the agreements, consideration should be given to re-negotiation with either the user or supplier representative or both.

Other factors

As well as those examples given above, there will be other items to be included, depending upon, among other things, the type of services being delivered, the organisation, its business sector and environment.

3.6 Producing the documents

When the specification phase is completed the IT directorate has successfully transformed business demands to IT deliverables. At this stage the service level requirements are produced and consequently the specsheets are filled in and agreed upon. It is now clear what customers want and what are the implications to the IT directorate in terms of how they can deliver the requested services. In this phase the formal documents can be produced

3.6.1 The Service Catalogue

The Service Catalogue gives an overview of the services that the IT directorate can provide to its customers and, as such is a major marketing tool. Producing a Service Catalogue provides an excellent opportunity to create a distinct profile of the IT directorate. In this way the IT directorate can present itself as a service provider and show their customers what they actually do.

The Service Catalogue contains details of all the services that the IT directorate is able to provide. In this sense the catalogue can also help the IT directorate to bridge the knowledge gap between the IT and the business organisation. The Service Catalogue can therefore be used to manage the expectations that customers have of an IT services organisation. Maintaining realistic customer expectations will lead to a considerably easier process of negotiation.

When designing the Service Catalogue the following pointers should be kept in mind:

- avoid technical language, instead use the language of the business that the customer understands

- think as a customer, then decide what is interesting to them and what is not

- spend time and effort on the layout of the document, it is the marketing document of the IT directorate

- catalogues need not necessarily be (only) paper based but may be made available electronically, for example as part of the company intranet services, or on CD-ROM.

3.6.2 Service Level
Agreement

The format of the SLA depends on a number of variables including:

- physical aspects of the organisation
  - size
  - complexity
  - geographical distribution

- cultural aspects
  - number of languages used
  - relationship between IT suppliers and customer
  - charging policy
  - homogeneity

- type of business
  - legal constraints
  - operating timeframes – eg nine to five or twenty-four hours.

Many businesses nowadays are organised in quite independent business units or profit centres. In these kind of structures the IT directorate should treat these entities as separate customers.

SLA structures

When introducing SLAs into organisations it is best practice to deal with common issues once, rather than engage in similar negotiations several times. Although there are many ways of 'cutting the cake', practical experience has shown that however the assembling of SLA elements is addressed, the result is invariably one of three levels of SLA. Some examples of the ways different organisations have adapted a 3-level approach are given here, but this is not an exhaustive list, the correct way of establishing multi-level SLAs is for them to reflect the organisation of the customer. Remember that we are dealing with people, not machines. The key in establishing good SLAs is to see them as agreements between people, not agreements about computing – ie keep the process customer focused.

Hierarchical structure

A single service is to be available to customers throughout a country, at a range of establishments of different sizes, work patterns and work intensity.

1. Some general parameters were established once, centrally – availability hours, security requirements, screen and access options. These basic parameters for the service were agreed once, and signed off at a very high level. (In fact in this real life example they were signed at such a high level, only one signature was needed – the executive signing was responsible both for the operational work and the IT services!)

2. For each type of site, a committee representing similar sites agreed SLA terms covering them all.

3. Only at the lowest level were discussions held at each site, by which time most of the parameters for the service and its delivery were already established.

Network services

A multi-national organisation has several LANs in each of its large office sites, all are linked.

1. Availability of the 'backbone' services and email is common to all customers and agreed once.

2. Within that availability and performance constraint, agreement is reached at site or operational division level to cover the requirements of that group or type of customer.

3. At the lowest level SLAs for specific, mostly bespoke, services are negotiated.

Business Groupings

1. Corporate level: general rules, guidelines or terms of delivery that apply to all customers and all services. This might include general help desk services, charging policy, penalty clauses.

2. Customer level: rules and guidelines that apply to all services for one particular customer. The use of this level naturally depends on the differentiation of the customer group.

3. Service level: customer and service specific quality targets, thresholds etc that apply to one service for one specific customer.

Penalty Clauses

Where IT services are formally charged for, many organisations have opted to include provision for financial penalty clauses within SLAs, to be invoked when service targets are not achieved. Strong and impassioned arguments both for and against penalty clauses are often heard, in practice it would seem that their appropriateness is often a reflection more of an organisation's culture than an element of good (or bad) service level management practice.

The expression of such clauses is fairly easy, with financial penalties being fixed against agreed and measurable objectives, often with a percentage of the charges abated for failure to meet the targets. The concept can also be extended to provide for bonus payments if targets are achieved or exceeded, or for penalties against the customer if their parts of the SLA are not kept, for example if agreed throughput is exceeded.

Reservations about the use of a penalty clause cite that it is in most cases in neither party's interest to receive money instead of the required service. Often a penalty clause stands in the way of a constructive solution for the problem at hand, with concentration on fault and finding a party to blame rather than re-establishing service levels. Often an IT directorate feels obliged to direct efforts at 'waterproofing' the contract instead of delivering the best quality service possible.

One alternative to financial penalties is to consider establishing an escalation clause. Should IT services not be delivered as agreed, a higher management level end informed. In this way, the managerial hierarchy in the organisation resolves disputes. The key of the escalation clause is to bring the concerns to the attention of the management level with the authority to actually solve them.

> Example: the performance of email for a certain customer unit is below the agreed standard. User complaints to the help desk are logged, but problem management fails to detect the root cause. User management is informed and a meeting with the service manager is planned. In this meeting a series of actions is agreed. The IT department will supply a network engineer to investigate the problem and will report on progress within one week. Meantime, the problem spreads and other customer units are affected. The connectivity of the entire company is threatened. Senior management is involved and the item is on the agenda for the regular meeting with the IT director. At this level, there is authority to quickly form an expert team with a skilled external professional.

Techniques

When developing and introducing SLAs in general the following pointers constitute good general advice.

Keep SLAs simple
External documents should be easily accessible and should invite the customer to read them. In management terms this means typically no more than two pages of A4 per service component.

Do not be over ambitious
Not all your problems with understanding and communicating with business customers will be solved by introducing service level management. The goal should be to create an environment where discussing facts is possible, instead of discussing feelings. A discussion based on facts can lead to a solution; a discussion based solely on feelings leads most times to the dissatisfaction of one or both parties.

Save the technology related aspects for the internal documents
The best SLAs, like the best ships, keep the technical elements and the driving mechanism out of sight 'below the waterline'. While there may well be a place for technical detail in internal documents, keep external documents readable for the customer. Use technical shorthand only when you are certain that all parties will readily understand it.

Develop a standard SLA model
Standard models have two major advantages, they are easier to read and less difficult to maintain. (People, both users and maintainers get used to looking for and finding particular information in particular places.) The maintainability of the SLA will be a major factor in its usefulness over time.

Review the effectiveness and the efficiency on a regular basis
As with any process the success of service level management depends on its ability to adjust to new goals and demands of the customer. The earlier described 'market-in' approach to delivering IT services requires a constant and close monitoring of the process.

Don't agree to anything that you cannot monitor
If it cannot be measured in a way that both customer and supplier can understand, then any agreement to supply is meaningless.

3.6.3 Underpinning contracts

All underpinning contracts have to be reviewed. This review may lead to re-negotiating the contract. Underpinning contracts have to be easily accessible for all participants in the service level management process. The use of a document reference list as described when defining service requirements (section 3.4) can contribute to the accessibility of underpinning contracts.

Underpinning services supplied in-house are also vital to the service and it is as important to review these and, if they are not already in place, introduce Operational Level Agreements to safeguard the supporting service.

4   The Service Quality Plan

A specific issue of service level management is the management of agreed service levels. Once these are agreed they should be monitored for compliance. The management of service levels is built on agreeing measurable, but customer focused, services and controlling achievements to ensure service levels are met.

To be able to manage the agreed service levels it is essential to have a full overview of IT service provision. It concerns the IT service capabilities, the agreed service levels and therefore demands for the external and internal service suppliers. The information required to manage, gathered together and held in a consistent and compatible format is referred to here as the Service Quality Plan.

This chapter offers guidance about the development of the Service Quality Plan and to define the who, where and when of delivering and controlling the services at an operational level.

4.1   Introduction to the Service Quality Plan

The Service Quality Plan is the ultimate quality assurance tool. The Service Quality Plan balances customer service requirements with the organisation structure of the IT services organisation. To achieve this, the Service Quality Plan consists of process parameters that are set for the service and systems management processes in the structure of the IT services organisation.

The Service Quality Plan puts together all the management information that is needed to successfully manage an IT service department. For each service management process that is put in place process parameters are defined. An example is the incident management process, where reaction or incident solving times and impact levels are determined. Some example process parameters are shown in Table 1.

The Service Quality Plan consists of performance indicators for the service management processes. These are derived from the service requirements and are specified in the internal specsheets. This procedure is explained in Chapter 3 *Quantifying IT Services*.

The Service Quality Plan is the crucial document needed to successfully manage an IT services organisation. The Service Quality Plan also defines management reporting. It is important to define:

- what the report will contain

- when the report will be produced (frequency)

- at whom the report is targeted.

Some examples are given in Table 2, below.

Capacity management	Configuration management
Maximum processor usage per server 50%	98% of CIs are correct in CMDB
Maximum occupied disk space per server 85%	All CI changes go through change management
Maximum memory usage per server 85%	
Maximum size swap file per server 250% of disk space	**Incident management**
Maximum usage of line capacity per LAN 50%	Availability of help desk on working days from 08.30 to 17.00 hours.
Maximum transaction volume 65% of maximum volume of agreed service level	Maximum waiting period on Help Desk telephone 2 minutes

Table 1: Example process parameters

Configuration management report	Frequency	Target audience
Overview of performed changes	monthly	Configuration Manager
Audit of configuration management process	quarterly	Configuration Manager Service Level Manager
Incident Management Report	**Frequency**	**Target audience**
Overview of incidents not closed in time	weekly	Problem Manager Availability Manager
Overview of incidents which affected more than 10 users	daily	Availability Manager Problem Manager Service Level Manager
Overview of total number of incidents by category and impact	monthly	Service Level Manager Problem Manager
Overview of escalated incidents, problems, mean times to service recovery	monthly	Problem Manager Availability Manager

Table 2: Example of reports against targets

4.2 Internal targets

If an agreement is reached on service levels for the customer, internal targets have to be defined to be able to deliver these agreements. Internal targets are defined in the specsheet service.

Internal targets support the external targets with a given margin. This margin allows the IT services organisation to use extra time for corrective actions like scheduling, redefine the workload or use extra quality checks, adjustments of external and internal targets, training personnel. Internal targets are agreed for every party that takes part in delivering the service.

> IT has, in the subject of internal and external targets, something to learn from traditional engineering techniques. In production engineering, one would expect corrective action to take place when variation from specification reached, say, 50% of the allowed tolerance, giving time to reset machinery without interrupting supply or producing unacceptable products. From civil engineering we can learn the merits of testing products to determine how they might react when loaded several times in excess of their designed specification.

As an example the typical delivery of a workstation is described.

> The SLA guarantees the workstation to be delivered within 2 weeks. The workstation consists of a certain type of personal computer, network connection, default installed operating software and office suite, network password and storage on the LAN for saving documents etc. The timescale is:
> * the purchase of the PC takes 1 week
> * the installation of hardware is done by the Technical support team within 1 day of receiving the PC
> * the software is installed by Software support team with a remote support system and takes 2 days
> * the definition of a network user and the default storage space on the LAN system is done by the LAN support team within 2 days but can be done right after receiving the request for change
> * the network connection is created by the technical support team after the installation of software and also takes 1 day.
>
> The total time for delivering the workstation is 1 week and 4 days. The margin for this delivery is 1 day (with a work week containing only 5 days). If there is an error or extra work has to be scheduled this day can be used.

Whereas external targets are customer focused and are defined in functional terms, internal targets are focused on the IT services organisation's internal structure and are typically specified in technical terms.

Examples of specification of internal targets for the IT infrastructure include:

- CPU power

- Mb internal memory

- usage of CPU hours

- escalation times in days, hours or minutes

- storage defined in Mb or Gb

- workload in MIPS

- maximum number of users per shared resource

- maximum number of concurrent users

- installation procedures for hardware, operating software and application software

- office suite containing, word processor, spreadsheet program and presentation software

- network response times

- number of tapes or cartridges

- number of lines (asynchronous/synchronous)

- number of ISDN connections

- backup and maintenance times

- reliability in maximum number of errors allowed per time span

- availability in percentage of the service hours.

Typical examples of specification of internal targets for applications development and support include:

- delivery dates

- performance issues in seconds

- capacity requirements in terms of MIPS, Mb etc

- functional acceptance criteria

- reliability in maximum number of errors allowed per time span

- availability in percentage of the service hours

- support issues in covering times to fix faults according to their severity

- help desk diagnostic scripts

- procedures for fixing functional, performance or security problems

- support documentation

- cost; charging rates, day rates etc.

The goal of using internal targets is to guarantee the agreed service levels. They are in practice neither legally binding nor enforceable, but they do allow management to establish the components of services and to manage the achievement of agreed service levels.

The Service Quality Plan should always adhere to the latest SLAs. To manage this the Service Quality Plan must contain a release number and date. The reason for update should be recorded.

A rough outline of a Service Quality Plan is given in Annex D.

| 4.3 | Underpinning contracts | If external suppliers are involved in the delivery of the IT services, underpinning contracts must be drawn up to support the service levels agreed in SLAs. |

Underpinning contracts must be reviewed to ensure that they support the service levels. If not, the contract should be re-negotiated. It is likely that extra costs will be incurred to realise higher support levels from the supplier. The Service Level Manager usually needs to discuss these issues with the customer organisation so they may jointly decide whether these costs are justifiable.

Whereas SLAs are often defined at three levels, it is usual for underpinning contracts to be made at only one level. This means the advantage of scale can be used to come to a more cost-effective contract. The IT services organisation then has to accumulate the service levels over different customers to come to an underpinning contract.

**4.4   Operational level
agreements**

In typical large IT service organisations operational level
agreements (OLA) can be used to underpin the support
of the service levels agreed in SLAs.

OLAs are derived from the specsheet service for internal
use and are set up as an agreement between two parties.
The procedure for reviewing the OLAs is similar to the
procedure for underpinning contracts.

Figure 13 shows an overview of the relationship between
SLA and underpinning contracts or operational level
agreements.

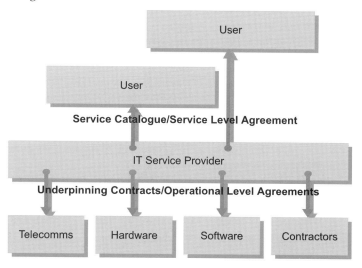

*Figure 13: The relationship between SLAs and underpinning
contracts or OLAs*

**4.5   Defining the Service
Quality Plan**

The Service Quality Plan defines the targets for internal
providers. The specification of internal targets in the
Service Quality Plan is done as described in Chapter 3
Quantifying IT services and combines the description of
the aspects for external as well as internal use as given
for the services specsheet.

It is recommended that the specifications for all internal
providers be defined in one integral Service Quality Plan.
It is essential that providers have an overview of their
activities, as a part of the whole service delivery.
Defining one Service Quality Plan for the whole
organisation enables every provider to be aware of
everyone's actions.

The definition of the Service Quality Plan is the responsibility of the Service Level Manager. If the organisation has a dedicated Quality Manager, then the Service Quality Plan may well be co-ordinated into the organisation's quality plan. The Service Level Manager, in any case, works closely with the organisation's quality initiatives since they will support the concepts of service level management.

Figure 14 shows the activity flow of defining and maintaining a Service Quality Plan.

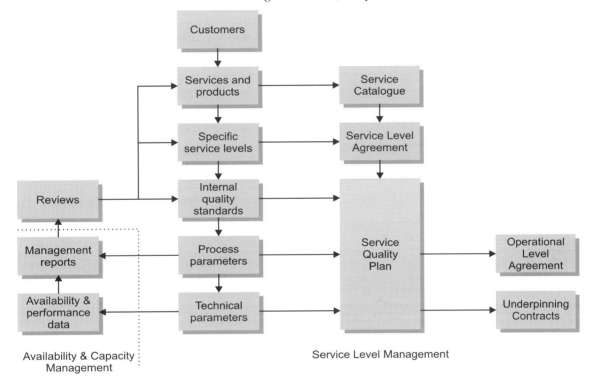

Figure 14: defining and maintaining a Service Quality Plan

| 4.6 | **Building the Service Quality Plan document** |

The Service Quality Plan document is the written definition of the internal targets, the responsibilities and internal delivery times that are necessary to live up to the agreed service levels.

The Service Quality Plan document consists essentially of the total set of specsheets service for internal and external use categorised per internal provider or service. To complete the document the responsibilities are defined and a summarised total of services and service components are given per internal provider. Where services are provided externally the underpinning contract is mentioned and summarised.

For producing the Service Quality Plan document the ISO9000 standards can be used.

The following aspects might be a part of the Service Quality Plan document:

- mission statement (purpose of the Service Quality Plan)

- document control (release number, date and reason, control procedures, management approval)

- distribution issues

- management and maintenance responsibilities

- definition, maintenance and review strategy and procedures

- description of IT service and support organisation

- internal audit procedures

- management reporting procedures

- training and education policy

- corrective actions procedures

- specification of services (specsheets) for internal and external use.

A skeleton Service Quality Plan can be found in Annex D.

4.7 Maintaining the Service Quality Plan

The maintenance of the Service Quality Plan is driven by the changes in the Service Catalogue or SLAs and management reporting from availability and capacity management.

Changes in the Service Catalogue or SLA may lead to changes in the specifications for the service provider. These changes lead to a change in the specsheet services. The Service Quality Plan is defined to ensure and manage the agreed service levels, so if services change the Service Quality Plan has to be reviewed.

Other maintenance of the Service Quality Plan may come from the reporting of the availability and capacity management processes. Reviews of service achievements may lead to adjustments in the Service Catalogue or SLAs (if the defined services and levels do not adhere to the current situation). Reviews of service achievements may also lead to adjustments in internal targets (ie the internal targets do not support the agreed service levels).

If service achievements are not compliant with the agreed service levels a service improvement programme must be started to ensure that the achievements are compliant in future. If agreed service levels turn out to be non-compliant with the current usage the Service Catalogue and SLAs must be adjusted. Also service improvement programmes may be started if achievements turn out to be on a higher level then agreed. Eventually this may lead to adjustments in the Service Catalogue and the SLAs.

The Service Quality Plan contains the parameters, targets and techniques upon which the quality of delivered service rests, thus the performance and reputation of the Service Level Manager is dependent upon the effective and timely maintenance of the plan. Where there is a Quality Manager within the organisation, day-to-day maintenance may be their responsibility, but responsibility for the results of the plan are inseparable from the responsibilities of the Service Level Manager.

A Further information and associated guidance

Useful contacts

This book forms part of the IT Infrastructure Library (ITIL). It has been written to form a part of an integrated set of guidance, each book addressing some aspect of IT service management. Some books, of which this is one, describe best practice for a specific IT service management function, while others address more general IT service management issues, such as planning and organisation, or offer complementary guidance including case studies, guidance on using ITIL ideas in smaller units or network service management.

ITIL is managed on behalf of CCTA by Stichting EXIN, the Examination Institute for Information Science. CCTA, the UK government's Central Computer and Telecommunications Agency, who developed the ITIL guidance, remain the owners of the ITIL books and the ITIL trademarks.

The ITIL books themselves are only one part of the 'ITIL philosophy'. The guidance within the books is supported and complemented by training, qualifications, consultancy, software tools and seminars. Information on any aspect of ITIL is available from:

EXIN
4 Princes Street
Norwich NR1 3AZ
United Kingdom
Tel: (+44/0) 1603 610900
fax: (+44/0) 1603 617070
email: itil@exin.nl

An ITIL home page carries news, information and links for those interested in IT service management, and can be found at **www.exin.nl/itil.** The latest information on contacts can be found there.

Information on the range of ITIL-based qualifications in IT service management is available from these examination organisations:

Stichting EXIN
Postbus 191947
3501 DC Utrecht
Netherlands
Tel: (+31/0) 30 2344811
Fax: (+31/0) 30 2344850
email: itil@exin.nl

Information Systems Examination Board
1 Sanford St
Swindon SN1 1HJ
UK
Tel: (+44/0) 1793 417417
fax: (+44/0) 1793 480270
email: iseb@bcs.org.uk

Books can provide useful ideas, but experience has shown how helpful it can be to discuss issues with like minded individuals and organisations who are, or have been, in similar situations. This is one of the many benefits available from the organisations affiliated to ITSMF International. Originally established in the UK as a user group for ITIL, these organisations offer an invaluable forum for their members; including seminars and annual conferences, discounts for members etc. Affiliated organisations are:

For Southern Africa
ITSMF
PO Box 69362
Bryanston 2021
South Africa
Tel: (+27/0) 11 8071080

For Netherlands
ITIMF
Postbus 1260
3890 BB Zeewolde
Netherlands
Tel: (+31/0) 36 5224752
email: itimf@pi.net

For UK and elsewhere
ITSMF
1A Taverners Square
Silver Road
Norwich NR3 4SY
Tel: (+44/0) 1603 767181
email:
itsmf@gtnet.gov.uk

At the time of writing (September 1997) ITSMF International is working with local ITIL supporters to initiate new ITSMF organisations in Australia, German speaking Europe and the USA. Latest details can always be found via the ITIL home page.

B   Bibliography

The following ITIL books have been referred to during the writing of this book:

- *Availability Management*
  ISBN: 0 11 330551 6

- Business Continuity Management – An Introduction

- ISBN: 0 11 330669 5

- Business Continuity Management – A Guide to
  ISBN: 0 11 330675 X

- Capacity Management
  ISBN: 0 11 330544 3

- Change Management
  ISBN: 0 11 330525 7

- Configuration Management
  ISBN: 0 11 330530 3

- Contingency Planning
  ISBN: 0 11 330524 9

- Cost Management for IT Services
  ISBN: 0 11 330547 8

- Customer Liaison
  ISBN: 0 11 330546 X

- Help Desk
  ISBN: 0 11 330522 2

- Managing Supplier Relationships
  ISBN: 0 11 330562 1

- Problem Management
  ISBN: 0 11 330527 3

- Third Party and Single Source Maintenance
  ISBN: 0 11 330540 0

All of these books will be revised and replaced as part of the 'ITIL update' exercise during 1998/1999.

C Glossary

C.1 Acronyms

BCM	Business Continuity Management.
CPU	Central Processing Unit.
Gb	Gigabyte.
IP	Internet Protocol.
ISEB	Information Systems Examination Board
ISDN	Integrated Systems Data Network.
ISO	International Standards Organisation.
IT	Information Technology.
ITIL	IT Infrastructure Library.
ITIMF	IT Infrastructure Management Forum.
ITSM	IT Service Management.
ITSMF	IT Service Management Forum.
LAN	Local Area Network.
Mb	Megabyte.
MIPS	Millions of Instructions Per Second.
OLA	Operational Level Agreement.
PC	Personal Computer.
RFC	Request For Change.
SLA	Service Level Agreement.
SLM	Service Level Management.
SLR	Service Level Requirement.
SQP	Service Quality Plan.
WAN	Wide Area Network.

C.2 Definitions

Customer	The recipient of the IT service; usually the customer will have responsibility for the cost of the IT service, either directly through charging or indirectly in terms of demonstrable business need.
External target	One of the measures against which a delivered IT service is compared, expressed in terms of the customer's business.

Hard charging	Descriptive of a situation where, within an organisation, actual funds are transferred from the customer to the IT directorate in payment for the delivery of IT services.
Help desk	The single point of contact within the IT directorate for users of IT services.
Incident	An operational event which is not part of the standard operation of a system. It will impact on the system, although this may be slight and may even be transparent to users.
Internal target	One of the measures against which supporting processes for the IT service are compared. Usually expressed in technical terms relating directly to the underpinning service being measured.
ISO9001	The internationally accepted set of standards concerning quality management systems.
IT directorate	That part of an organisation charged with developing and delivering the IT services.
Operational level agreement	An internal agreement covering the delivery of services which support the IT directorate in their delivery of services.
Service achievement	The actual service levels delivered by the IT directorate to a customer within a defined time-span.
Service catalogue	Written statement of IT services, default levels and options.
Service improvement programme	A formal project undertaken within an organisation to identify and introduce measurable improvements within a specified work area or, work process.
Service level agreement	Written agreement between an IT service provider and the customer that documents agreed service levels for an IT service.
Service level management	The process of defining, agreeing, documenting and managing the levels of customer IT service, that are required and cost justified.
Service quality plan	The written plan and specification of internal targets designed to guarantee the agreed service levels.
Specsheet	Specifies in detail what the customer wants (external) and what consequences this has for the service provider (internal) such as required resources and skills.
Underpinning contract	A contract with an external supplier covering delivery of services that support the IT directorate in their delivery of services.
Waterline	The lowest level of detail relevant to the customer.

D   Skeletons

This annex contains a set of example skeleton documents that can be used as a basis for developing the documents required for service level management.

D.1   Project plan

A skeleton for the planning and implementation of the service level management process. The Project Plan also covers the first definition of the service catalogue, an initial service level agreement (the pilot SLA) and service quality plan.

The first phase of the project is the feasibility study. This should investigate the risks, costs and critical success factors for the implementation and execution of service level management. Section 1.7 *Benefits, costs and possible problems* offers guidance to execute the feasibility study. The feasibility study assures initial management commitment and budget for the planning and implementation of service level management. For the project plan the following skeleton can be used.

Header information and contents
> Version number, date created, date amended.
> Table of contents.

Release management
> Maintenance: who is responsible for the maintenance of the project plan?
> Distribution: how and when are new releases distributed?
> History: Release number and issue date.

Signatures
> Specification and signature of the manager responsible for the issue of the project assignment (eg IT Services Manager) and the Project Manager (eg Service Level Manager).

Introduction
> The goal of the project plan and reference to any documentation used.

Project assignment and terms
- Problem definition.
- Assignment.
- Results and deliverables.
- Project specific terms.
- Risk analysis.
- Project management:
  - time
  - money
  - quality
  - information
  - organisation.

Project organisation
- Responsibilities and staffing.
- Project manager.
- Project team (key professionals).
- Project support.
- Meeting structure, agenda and schedule.
- Management reports (project internal and external).

Activities

No	Description	Responsible	Duration	Effort	Schedule
1	**Planning**				
1.1	Appoint the Service Level Manager				
1.2	Define and agree the service level management goal				
1.3	Define and agree the roles, tasks and responsibilities				
1.4	Define and agree the scope of services and the process				
1.4.1	Specify Service Level Requirements				
1.4.2	Specify external targets				
1.4.3	Specify internal targets				
1.5	Define and agree the SLA structure				
1.6	Define and agree the negotiation and approval structure				
1.7	Define the model SLA				
1.8	Define the quality parameters				
1.9	Define priorities				
1.10	Define customer organisations and suppliers				
1.11	Define the relationships with other processes				
1.12	Define and agree on the service level management process				
1.13	Define and agree on the service level management procedures				
1.14	Evaluate supporting tools				
1.15	Define and agree on the communication plan				
1.16	Define and agree on the implementation plan				
2	**Implementation**				
2.1	Start the awareness campaign (initiation phase)				
2.2	Start negotiations with customer organisations				
2.3	Start specification of services and defining the Service Catalogue				
2.4	Define and agree on the Service Quality Plan				
2.5	Review underpinning contracts				
2.6	Establish and start SLM procedures				
2.7	Create a model Service Level Agreement				
2.8	Start the SLA pilot Negotiate Define Contract Monitor Review Report				
2.9	Evaluate the SLA pilot				
2.10	Start other SLA definitions				

Project planning overview
 GANTT and PERT charts.

D.2   Role description Service Level Manager

The nature and content of role descriptions varies between organisations. For many jobs, the role description comprises elements related to different roles undertaken by an individual. This role description, relating to service level management responsibilities, is presented as an example only; intended to illustrate the anticipated range of tasks, relevant skills and experience appropriate for the Service Level Manager.

The specific clauses used in this example will need adapting to any particular organisation's size, working practices and procedures.

Job title: Service Level Manager
Main duties

- Responsible for creating and maintaining the service catalogue.

- Formulates, negotiates and maintains the SLA structure.

- Negotiates the initial contents for each SLA.

- Analyses and reviews all achieved service levels and conducts comparison with the SLA.

- Catalogues, reviews and where appropriate renegotiates (or causes to be renegotiated) all underpinning contracts and operational level agreements.

- Reports the service achievements to the customer and IT service providers' management.

- Maintains links with the customers of the IT services, including chairing regular formal meetings to discuss the service achievements and future changes.

- Initiates actions necessary to improve or maintain levels of service.

- Prepares for and conducts regular reviews of SLAs with the customer organisations and negotiates and agrees any amendments necessary.

- Negotiates and maintains the requests for service (demand management).

- Prepares for and co-ordinates the audits and reviews of the service level management process and reports to the IT services manager.

- Liaises with other ITSM and IT functions.

- Keeps up to date with appropriate developments, in IT generally, in IT service management and in the organisation's business and policies.

- Ensures staff are adequately trained and encourages them to maintain up-to-date knowledge in all relevant areas.

Skills and experience required
The successful Service Level Manager is likely to benefit from the following:

- experience in service management

- general IT and business knowledge

- awareness of business culture and customer attitudes

- communication and negotiation skills

- patience and resilience.

It is all too easy to list skills desirable for any role to the extent that it looks unsuitable for any normal human being. The above list is therefore deliberately short, naturally many other skills are desirable, but the lack of any of the above is likely to make the task considerably more difficult. Note also the separation of service management and IT skills, experience of formalised customer-supplier relationships from outside the IT environment can be every bit as relevant.

Qualifications
ISEB/EXIN qualifications are based upon ITIL and the managers' certificate will demonstrate a knowledge of the principles of IT service management. The practitioner certificate in service level management will show the holder has skills and knowledge directly related to the task in hand.

D.3 Service Catalogue

The Service Catalogue defines the default services provided with the default levels and the options. The Service Catalogue can be used to give the customer organisation a profile of the IT service provider and it can give the users an overview of all services provided.

This section gives a rough outline of the contents of such a catalogue. The content and structuring shown here are equally applicable whether the Service Catalogue is a paper or electronic product.

1   Contents

Version number, date created, date amended.

Table of contents.

2   Foreword

The foreword introduces the Service Catalogue to the users. It is recommended that the Director of IT or the General Manager write the foreword. This shows the management commitment that is essential for the success of the service catalogue and the service level management process in general.

3   IT service provider profile

A short overview of the IT services organisation, mission statement and marketing concept. The profile should be customer focused. The profile is needed to get the trust and confidence of the users.

4   Service times and accessibility of the IT service provider

An overview of the service times and the front-office parts of the IT service provider (eg help desk, change management, service level management) with locations, telephone numbers and email addresses. The Service Catalogue is designed to display the services and options of the IT services. It is important that users know who and where to turn to if they want to make use of the IT services.

5   Overview of services and products

Overview of all services and products. The overview should contain the following aspects per service type or product:

- customer focused service or product description
- specifications
- deliverables
- service times (the time span the service can be used)
- maintenance times (the time span the service can not be used because of maintenance activities)

- support times (the time span the service is supported by eg the help desk, technical staff or stand-by personnel)

- delivery times (the time span from the point of request until delivery of the service)

- quality targets (availability, reliability, usability, priority) with the given defaults, options and request or change procedure. The quality targets in the Service Catalogue are defined via the external quality targets

- requirements (the requirements that the user should deliver for the IT service provider to be able to deliver the requested service or product)

- request and change procedure.

6   Contingency

An explanation of the contingency policy of the IT service provider. Contingency of IT services has proven to be an important item for customer organisations. By stating an effective policy, supporting the business contingency policies, the IT service provider shows themselves to be an effective business partner.

7   Pricing and charging

If applicable the pricing options and charging defaults are defined (optionally per service or product).

8   Index and definitions

The Service Catalogue effectively forms the (internal) marketing brochure for the IT services unit, and is, at the very least, a major element of the marketing literature for the IT directorate as a whole. This should be kept firmly in mind when considering the design and content of the catalogue, especially for an organisation likely to be in competition with external IT suppliers in the near future. Possibly both paper and electronic version will be developed, designed to complement each other; for example an intranet version may incorporate examples and demonstrations, electronic request forms etc; a paper version might be restricted to a high level view. Whatever approach is taken, this as with all of service level management should be driven by an understanding and sympathy for the customers perspective, designed for their ease of comprehension rather than modelled on the IT directorate's internal structure and service offerings.

D.4   Service Level Agreement

An SLA specifies particular IT services and service levels for a customer organisation. This annex gives an outline to specify a Service Level Agreement.

1 Contents

Version number, date created, date amended
Table of contents.

2 Release management

Maintenance: who is responsible for the maintenance of the SLA?
Distribution: how and when are new releases distributed?
History: release number and issue date?

3 Signatures

Specification and signature of the IT service provider manager and the Business Manager. It should be defined for what period the SLA is agreed and when it will be revised.

4 Global statements

Global statements concerning the delivery of IT services and the responsibilities of the provider and the customer. This should contain the following:

- who to contact concerning this agreement

- who to contact when services are failing

- escalation procedures

- statements of penalties

- definitions.

5 Specification of parties

A short description of the IT service provider and the customer organisation.

6 Summary of responsibilities:

Summary of the responsibility of the parties and roles involved.

7 Specification of services

The services are specified with the agreed levels. The specification should contain:

- customer focused service or product description

- specifications

- deliverables

- service times (when the service can be used)

- maintenance times (when the service can not be used because of maintenance activities)

- support times (when the service is supported by eg the Help Desk, Technical staff or stand-by personnel)

- delivery times (time between request and delivery of the service)

- quality targets (availability, reliability, usability, priority) with the given defaults, options and request or change procedure. The quality targets in the Service Catalogue are defined via the external quality targets

- requirements (the requirements that the user should deliver for the IT service provider to be able to deliver the requested service or product)

- request and change procedure.

8   Management reporting

Specification of management reporting with the defined contents and delivery times.

9   Review procedure

The description of the procedure to review the SLA. This procedure must be agreed by the IT service provider as well as the customer organisation. The procedure must involve the scheduled dates for review, the regular review meetings and the change procedure for adjusting the SLA.

10 Index and definitions.

D.5   Service Quality Plan

The goal of the Service Quality Plan (SQP) is to support the control of service delivery. The service quality plan provides an overview as well as a detailed view of actions to be taken and parameters needed to deliver the services as agreed. The actions and parameters are described using specification sheets. These specification sheets are gathered in the SQP.

This annex gives a rough outline of the contents of such a Service Quality Plan.

1   Header and Content

Version number, date created, date amended

Table of contents.

2   Release management

Maintenance : who is responsible for the maintenance of the SQP?

Procedure : how is the SQP updated?

Distribution : how and when are new releases distributed and how are previous releases taken out of circulation?

History : release number and issue date?

Reason : reason for update.

3   Quality mission statement

A short description of the Quality Mission Statement of the IT service provider. The Service Quality Plan has to support this mission statement.

4   Responsibilities

An overview of management and staff with their responsibilities. This overview supports communication about service delivery.

5   Service providers

Overview of all, internal and external, service providers with a reference to the service they provide. For external providers it is recommended that a reference to the underpinning contract be made. When internal providers underpin the service via Operational Level Agreements a reference to these agreements should be made.

6   Service delivery overview

A overview of the service delivery actions and parameters per service. The overview will contain all actions for all service components and suppliers (internal and external). It is strongly recommended that the overview shows a process flow. This reinforces the understanding of all services, service components and actions per supplier.

7   Specification sheets services

Collection of all specification sheets.

8   Management reports

Contents, scheduling and distribution parameters for the management reports.

9   Reviews and quality assurances

Procedure, scope, scheduling and responsibilities for reviewing and assessing the Service Quality Plan.

10 Index and definitions.

D.6 Example service level requirements

The service that is described in this example is the network service. It is not said that every IT service provider should define a network service. For example an IT provider might consider the network as part of delivering overall functionality on the terminal (end to end service). However the example gives a fair idea of how the outlines of a service emerge and how the service can be designed.

Name service:	Network services		
Code service:	NS		
Customer liaison officer:	Chris Jones	Phone:	
IT liaison officer:	S L Manager	Phone:	

Expression of the customer need, including a precise description of the desired result
Users will, on request, be provided with a network connection. The network service gives users the possibility to make a physical connection from a client (own computer) to any other segment of the company local area network. This service is about connecting people and thereby improving the quality of internal communication.

Special instructions concerning the design of the service
None

At what time should the service be available
01/07/1998

Dates by which the following phases of the design have to be completed:

Specification of the service	24/04/1997
Specification of the service delivery	24/04/1997
Specification of the quality aspects	24/04/1997
Producing the service level agreement	01/05/1997

IT staff responsible for the design of the service

Team leader	
Team members	

IT staff involved with planning and executing the service

Information analysis	no
System development	no
Systems and network management	yes
Maintenance	yes
Support	yes

Reference to target operating procedures and quality targets

Average workload of the local area network may not exceed 30% of the total network capacity. The quality of the connection can be affected.

What service level agreement will be replaced

None – new service.

Signatures

IT services organisation

_____

Customer

_____

D.7 Example service specsheet

FOR EXTERNAL USE

General information

Date latest adjustment:	April 18th, 1997			
Name service:	Network services			
Code service:	NS			
Customer representative:	Manager sales department		Phone:	123
IT representative:	Head of IT		Phone:	777

Description of the service

Within the organisation there is electronic communication between computers, systems and printers. This communication is possible through a computer network. The network consists of cables, hubs, routers, bridges and patches. The network service is defined as the possibility to establish a connection. Therefore the availability of computers and/or systems is not part of the network service. A connection is provided by linking a client to the network and the issuing of an IP address. Network services consist of:

1   Local Area Network services (within buildings)

2   Wide Area Network services (national and global communication)

3   Remote Network services (connection with the company LAN through a telephone line).

Duration of the service

As long as the SLA is valid.

Service hours

On company working days from 08.00 to 18.00 hours.

Location where the service is provided

1   LAN: all offices.

2   WAN: all offices.

3   Remote: headquarters.

Financial consequences for the customer

Costs associated to network services are accounted for in the IT year budget. The costs for remote services will be charged on a direct individual bases.

Information, products and facilities to supplied by the customer

1   Name, telephone, department and manager.

2   A working PC and modem (if applicable).

Terms of delivery

The general terms of delivery apply.

Service levels (examples)
External target no. 1: availability

Target	The service is available during 95% of opening hours.
Criterion	The service is available if a connection is possible from one segment in the network to any other segment of the network.
How to measure, how to document and by whom	On request of the customer the Helpdesk employee can perfom a 'ping' test to establish the availability of the network service. This action will be documented in the service support tool.

External target no. 2: performance

Target	Performance of the network will comply to the industry target 10 Megabit.
	Additional standards: V32bis in addition to V42bis (error correction) will apply. Modems have a minimum baud rate of 14.400 bps.
Criterion	Compliance will be affirmed by external experts.
How to measure, how to document and by whom	Once in two years, or in case of severe performance problems, an external and neutral party will audit the infrastructure for compliance to the specified industry standards. The report will be presented to the head of the IT directorate.

Timetables

1   Time to service delivery: within two working days of the request being received by the IT directorate.

2   Service hours: regular company office hours. Outside these hours the service can be used, but acceptance criteria will not be guaranteed.

3   Waiting time: for remote network services a waiting time of 15 minutes to establish a connection is the maximum. This also applies outside office hours.

4   Processing time: processing time depends on the availability of a modem at the time the service is requested, but will not exceed 15 minutes.

Security, backup and recovery and contingency planning

1   Patch panels are locked and can only be accessed by IT personnel.

2   There is no contingency plan available for this service.

Procedures

Procedures required for signing the agreement

The head of the IT directorate and the Business Manager sales sign the Service Level Agreement, from which date the agreement is official.

Change procedure for the agreement

This agreement will be automatically extended for one year if, one month before the agreed expiry date, neither party has requested re-negotiation. Requests for changes to the agreement must be issued in writing to the IT directorate after which a negotiation with the contracting parties will take place within 10 working days.

Procedure for accepting the service

Help desk staff will verify if new users can use the service as defined in this agreement.

Procedure of service delivery

1 Customer representative initiates request for service to help desk.

2 Help desk records all the necessary information.

3 Help desk informs user within two days and verifies if the service is accepted.

Corrective action

If targets specified in this agreement are not met, the IT director is responsible for ensuring that, minimally, one of following corrective actions is taken:

1 adjustment of the service quality plan

2 providing additional training for employees

3 dealing with the corrections before the service is continued.

Signatories

Customer representative _____

Date: _____

Head of IT _____

Date _____

FOR INTERNAL USE

Reference to external targets and guidelines

Company-wide guidelines for security will be established. Please refer to the IT security plan for further specification.

1 Reference to public health standards
Not applicable.

2 Reference to public safety standards
Not applicable.

3 Reference to environmental standards
Not applicable.

4 Reference to privacy standards
Not applicable.

5 Reference to legal standards or legislation
Not applicable.

6 Reference to necessary insurance
Insurance aspects will be discussed at corporate level.

Date when service can be delivered

July 1st, 1997.

Financial consequences for the IT directorate

Efforts (estimated man hours ongoing)

Management activities	16 hours per week
Monitoring	2 hours per week
Maintenance	20 hours per week
Support	12 hours per week

Additional investments

Call in facility (modem rack)	US$
Contract with WAN provider	US$

Quality, quantity and availability of IT personnel

During service hours a network technician (certified network engineer) will be available. For support we refer to our free of charge help desk service. We need 2 network technicians (certified network engineers) who will work in shifts, so that the service hours can be guaranteed. Morning shift is from 08.00 to 13.00 hours. Evening shift from 13.00 to 18.00 hours. Total workload is estimated at 50 hours per week. Workload per shift is hence estimated at 100%.

External dependencies

Suppliers: There are no formal agreements with suppliers in case of technical network failures. There is no back-up power supply and so the continuity of the service depends on the uninterupted supply of electricity.

Facilities that influence the quality of the service

Network usage

Target	Average network usage should be less than 30% of the maximum capacity.
Criterion	Total number of packages per second as a percentage of the total network capacity.
How to measure	Continuous with AXON LAN servant. The network manager checks as a part of his daily routine.
Corrective action	Improve network capacity Tuning Workload management.

Length of cable segment

Target	Length of cable segment does not exceed 100 metres.
Criterion	Maximum cable length as specified in industrial target for twisted pair cables.
How to measure	Check before a new connection is provided.
Corrective action	Shorten distance between wall outlet and work station.

Procedure of delivery

If a new workstation is requested the technical possibility is evaluated. Please refer to the service request for hardware/software. The following items are checked for presence:

1   a wall outlet within 3 metres of the desktop

2   a free IP address

3   a free patch connection

4   a free connection to the hub.

E Self assessment

This annex contains a checklist to help in a self-assessment exercise, examining the service level management process for compliance and effectiveness. Such checks would normally be carried out once or twice a year.

The assessment should aim to verify whether activities in the service level management process:

- are executed in compliance with defined procedures

- are leading to the desired result.

The assessment should aim to improve the organisation, not to enforce the agreed procedures. If non-compliance to procedures is detected, the question why this occurred should always be addressed. This question will lead to one of the following answers, with appropriate measures:

Reason for non compliance	Countermeasure
Staff do not perceive the procedure as useful	Investigate the root cause and either: • improve staff awareness • improve procedure.
Staff perceive procedure as time consuming	Investigate the complaint and either: • trim down the procedure improve staff efficiency by training.
Procedure leads to wrong results	Verify and improve the procedure. Next investigate why this was not brought to management attention and either: • improve communication structure • improve awareness • show management commitment.
Procedure is simply neglected	Investigate how and why and involve staff concerned. Raise awareness.

E.1 Results

The key question is to compare targets with the results delivered. Clearly, verification of this area is 'above the waterline' and directly addresses customer satisfaction. The organisation must ask 'are we doing the right things?'

- are the SLAs negotiated with the customer organisations?

- are service achievements discussed with customer organisations?

- are escalation procedures followed if agreed service levels are not delivered?

- is the customer satisfied with the delivered service?

E.2 Compliance with procedures

Here the key question is the compliance of how things are done (everyday practice) with how they should be done (what is written down and formally agreed upon). This verification is 'below the waterline' and addresses the efficiency of the organisation – 'are we doing things the right way?'

Checklist

The following areas can be subject to checking:

- are staff aware of the service level management process?

- are explicit targets defined and monitored by management?

- are all IT services defined and documented?

- are SLAs defined?

- are SLAs reviewed with the customer regularly (check minutes)?

- are underpinning contracts and Operational Level Agreements defined?

- does the agreement structure conform to the Service Catalogue and SLAs?

- are changes in the IT Infrastructure managed in the light of the SLA?

- is the information defined in the Service Catalogue, Service Level Agreements and the Service Quality Plan general available for other processes?

- is the availability and capacity of the IT services monitored?

- are management reports generated and distributed

- are new IT services specified and quantified according to the procedures?

- is contingency planning involved in the defined service levels?

Input for the 'do it yourself' assessment is:

- service level management process description
- Service Catalogue
- all SLAs
- Service Quality Plan
- minutes of review discussions
- regular management reports
- exception reports concerning non-compliance to agreed service levels.

F Awareness campaign

Mounting a successful awareness campaign is one of the critical success factors in implementing a service level management process. Service level management is an activity which involves both the IT services organisation and the business departments (IT users or customers).

An awareness campaign should therefore be directed at:

- creating a customer understanding for the introduction and maintenance of agreed service levels

- motivating the customer organisation to take responsibility in the implementation and maintenance of service level management

- raising awareness amongst IT staff of quality control, customer focus etc.

When implementing service level management as a project, the awareness campaign will be a part of the overall project communications plan. During the preparation of the awareness campaign it is important to listen carefully to the customer organisation and to pinpoint their expectations of service level management. Remember after all, *Communication is the management of expectations*. If you know what your customer expects you can deliver a result accordingly. If you do not know what your customer expects, you can only succeed through luck.

The awareness campaign consists of two phases:

- the initiation phase – its purpose is to obtain commitment

- the motivation phase – its purpose is to retain that commitment and obtain co-operation during the implementation.

F.1   Initiation Phase

The initiation phase of the awareness campaign should run parallel to the preparation and planning of the project implementing service level management.

First the aims of the campaign must be defined. This depends on what are perceived as possible risks in the IT and customer environment. Sometimes merely explaining what will happen is enough. In most cases however, resistance to change must be overcome.

To identify the risks a list of stakeholders in the project is defined: senior management, middle management, IT staff, end users. Questions that need answering are:

- what are the possible consequences of the change for each group?

- what risks can be defined in each group?

- what amount of resistance can be expected?

- who may be allies in opposing or supporting the change?

Resistance can manifest itself in many ways. Some typical manifestations and frequently heard statements are listed below.

- It is impossible to find time for the project, perhaps because people are unwilling to make time – 'this is a matter of priority'.

- Misunderstanding and/or unwillingness. This can be caused by a perceived threat – 'I thought I was doing my job just fine' or by cynicism – 'I have seen this kind of thing before, why should it work any better this time?'

- Inflexible culture – 'we've always done it this way'.

- Lack of commitment to new ways of working – 'It's all nonsense. We have more important things to do. We have to make money'.

In the initiation phase the awareness campaign should be tailored to overcome identified resistance. For the project manager it is advisable to seek allies for his ideas up front.

> *A lonely cry in the desert is seldom heard and less often answered...*

Involve corporate communications professionals in the design of the awareness campaign. If they are not members of the project use them as advisors to the project team. The project manager may also consider employing an external specialist.

Commitment of senior management, as always, is important, both for the customer and the IT organisation. This commitment should clearly be demonstrated as part of the awareness campaign. Especially during the initiation phase the explicit commitment of senior management can act as a catalyst for change.

Means that can be used during the initiation phase are presentations by key personnel, attendance at seminars about service level management, participation in workshops and discussions and even the distribution of a newsletter, on paper or electronic, in which the progress of the project is monitored and reported.

F.2   The motivation phase

The motivation phase runs parallel to the implementation and post implementation phase of the service level management project. The motivation phase is aimed at maintaining the commitment of all stakeholders in the (post) implementation phase of the service level management project.

Information can in some cases be mistaken for propaganda, either by the sending or by the receiving party. To avoid this, the information that is needed to 'sell the idea' is best combined with information on 'how to make things work'. One example of this approach is combining a workshop on identifying user requirements with a short presentation on the meaning and consequences of the introduction of service level management.

Extensive scientific research in communication techniques has shown that:

- 20% of what people hear will be remembered
- 35% of what people see will be remembered
- 50% of what people hear and see will be remembered
- 80% of what people have put into practice will be remembered.

This information can be of use when selecting the means to communicate the message. However, means should only support what you have to say. They cannot replace the message!

F.2.1   The message

To successfully support the introduction of service level management the message should contain at least the following elements:

- The focus on a customer/supplier relationship between the users and the IT-organisation. Sometimes there is a free choice for the user, sometimes not, in either case customer satisfaction is the supplier's top priority.

- The only way to satisfy a customer is to understand what they want. Therefore customer demands have to be explicitly agreed upon in an objective and measurable way.

- The quality of the provided service has to be assured through a quality management system, where processes can be evaluated by measurable internal targets.

- The customer not only has rights, but obligations too. These thresholds should be an integrated part of the customer/supplier agreement.

- It is important that customers and IT staff are informed about the quality of the delivered IT services. Also an authoritative body has to be formed to take corrective actions when delivered IT services fail to meet the agreed standards.

- All stakeholders should have a clear perception of their role and responsibility in the ongoing service level management process.

F.2.2   The means

When selecting the means to communicate, the most important thing is of course to get the message across. It has already been said that means can only support the message, they can not replace it. When selecting means the following pointers should be kept in mind:

- Who is your target audience? Try to understand their expectations. It is often better to give two presentations than to mix two groups with different aims.

- Duration. A presentation that is too short is seldom a problem, a presentation too long can be perceived as boring or trivial. Don't try to tell everything there is to tell, try to focus on what is most important to your audience.

- Good engineering practice applies. Test an idea before you market it. Have texts reviewed by a third party, practice the presentations you're giving. In communication an important rule of thumb – preparing is 90%, doing is 10%.

Techniques for raising awareness

Presentations

Any presentation should comply with certain basic rules:

- the contents have to be understood by the audience
- the presentation should appeal to the audience
- choose a logical construction (from here to there, from simple to complex, from the present to the past or future, from specific to general, from concrete to abstract, chronological display of facts)
- agree actions, this will enforce the commitment you want.

Memos, notices

Written text can be very powerful. Keep the language simple and to the point. In most cases anything over one page is wasted. Remember that technical authoring is a recognised profession, do not underestimate the skills involved. Also bear in mind that, whilst a picture can be worth a thousand words, this is only true if it is the right picture.

Newsletters

Although sending out a regular newsletters can be effective, it is the technique most likely to fail, especially when time limits are pressing. Hastily produced and amateurish newsletters will send negative signals to the project stakeholders. The conclusion of waning management commitment is very easily made but not easily corrected. When introducing a newsletter make someone responsible for the (monthly) publication. Bear in mind that a newsletter should contain news and that it is not a newsletter for the newsletter's sake. Newsletters appeal to a wider public, so don't get lost in organisation-specific details. All of these points are equally applicable whether the newsletter is produced and distributed on paper or electronically, or posted as information on internet or intranet.

Personal contact, meetings

Keep in touch with key personnel, and regularly inform the project stakeholders. Especially involve persons or groups that may constitute a risk to the project. Remember that people who demonstrate resistance are by definition committed. If they were not they simply wouldn't care enough to resist. It is the job of the project manager to harmonise others' personal goals with the project's goals. Of course a less theoretical approach underpins this: if you can't beat them, join them.

Seminars, workshops

Attending seminars and workshops can be informative. In a workshop people are more actively involved than in a seminar, and people remember more information if they have put it into practice themselves. In addition results of a high quality workshop can be used for the project. Workshops are an extra chance to investigate what project stakeholders want.

G   Do's and don'ts of service level management

This annex gives a checklist of do's that help make service level management a success and don'ts that increase the risk of failure. The checklist provides a practical guidance and can be used during planning, implementation and the execution of the process.

G.1   Do's

- Do involve the customer's organisation as soon as possible.

- Do make the planning and implementation of service level management a joint effort between the IT service provider and the customer organisation (dual sponsorship).

- Do organise regular reviews to make the process more effective.

- Do organise independent audits to check compliance and to optimise the process make it more effective.

- Do specify that service requirements are customer focused and use the service quality plan to specify and communicate the internal requirements.

- Do treat customers' observations as facts.

- Do involve all departments in the service level management process. Make them your partners in providing services.

- Do agree only on qualified, quantified, measurable service levels.

- Do involve other service management and operational processes in delivering management reporting.

- Do keep wording as simple and clear as possible.

G.2   Don'ts

- Don't be over ambitious in setting formal service targets until all supporting processes and tools are implemented.

- Don't start defining an SLA before defining the process goal and activities.

- Don't agree to any target you cannot measure.

- Don't start by talking to your customer, start by listening.

- Don't tend to bureaucracy.

- Don't say NO! If a customer wants a service that you don't deliver normally, explain the consequences (time, money) if you do. Let the customer decide whether to invest.

Printed in the United Kingdom for The Stationery Office
J93874 C7 10/99 10170

The Stationery Office

Published by The Stationery Office and available from:

The Publications Centre
(mail, telephone and fax orders only)
PO Box 276, London SW8 5DT
Telephone orders/General enquiries 0870 600 5522
Fax orders 0870 600 5533

www.tso-online.co.uk

The Stationery Office Bookshops
123 Kingsway, London WC2B 6PQ
020 7242 6393 Fax 020 7242 6394
68-69 Bull Street, Birmingham B4 6AD
0121 236 9696 Fax 0121 236 9699
33 Wine Street, Bristol BS1 2BQ
0117 926 4306 Fax 0117 929 4515
9-21 Princess Street, Manchester M60 8AS
0161 834 7201 Fax 0161 833 0634
16 Arthur Street, Belfast BT1 4GD
028 9023 8451 Fax 028 9023 5401
The Stationery Office Oriel Bookshop
18-19 High Street, Cardiff CF1 2BZ
029 2039 5548 Fax 029 2038 4347
71 Lothian Road, Edinburgh EH3 9AZ
0131 228 4181 Fax 0131 622 7017

The Stationery Office's Accredited Agents
(see Yellow Pages)

and through good booksellers